Robert Carrier is one of the world's most famous food writers. One-time Food Editor of *The Sunday Times*, *Harper's Bazaar*, *Vogue* and *The Daily Telegraph Magazine*, he is the author of several important cook books – *Great Dishes of the World*, *The Robert Carrier Cookbook*, *The Robert Carrier Cookery Cards* and *Cooking For You*.

Also by Robert Carrier and available from Sphere
Great Dishes of the World
The Robert Carrier Cookery Course
    Volumes One, Two, Three and Five

Volume Four

The Robert Carrier
Cookery Course

Sphere Books Limited
30/32 Gray's Inn Road, London WC1X 8JL

First published in Great Britain by
W H Allen and Co Ltd 1974

Sphere Books edition published in 1976

Set in 10pt Bembo, 1pt leaded
Printed in England by Hazell Watson & Viney Ltd,
Aylesbury, Bucks

To Helena Radecka – 'Queen Bee' of my London Test Kitchen where all these recipes were dreamed up, tried out, re-tested and then perfected; to Caroline Liddell, Hilary Colbourn and Norma and Christopher Hillier – the expert choppers, stirrers, mixers, saucemakers and bakers; to Gunther Schlender and Terry Boyce, head chefs of my two restaurants, *Carrier's* in London and *Hintlesham Hall* in Suffolk, who lent their professional support; and to Jacqueline Cottee – my Personal Assistant for thirteen years – and Chief Taster – all my grateful thanks for their many years of effort on my behalf. It's been a lot of fun. And, more important, it's a great book.

Contents

Volume four

Volume five

Introduction

Cooking is easy; wonderfully easy. And cooking is fun. I firmly believe that every meal we have should be a pleasure, an adventure. And by that I do not mean that we all have to eat complicated dishes and rich sauces every day of our lives; nor do we have to spend all day in the kitchen to prepare the family dinner. But I do believe that we must take advantage of our meal times to produce well-planned, well-presented meals that are delicious to eat.

I personally would much rather have a lightly boiled egg and a perfectly dressed green salad than all the slap-dash meals in the world. And I want variety in my everyday eating. Of course, you'll say 'with two restaurants – one in London and the other in the country – his life is easy'. But you have no idea how, after a lot of entertaining and being entertained, I long for a simple grilled steak and a baked potato. Or, without a thought for the spreading waistline, a plate of steaming hot spaghetti or noodles tossed with fresh butter and grated Parmesan cheese.

My favourite foods are basically simple foods: lightly grilled chicken with mustard and ginger; a Provençal vegetable salad bathed in olive oil and lemon juice flavoured with finely chopped anchovies, sweet onion and fresh herbs; baby lamb chops, marinated with olive oil and dry white wine and then grilled over the open fire; tiny 'pillows' of cheese, crisp fried on the outside and deliciously creamy within. Or, for supper, a slice of home-made *pâté*, and a crisp green salad redolent of fruity olive oil. Add then, the simple luxuries: *gratin dauphinois* (thinly sliced potatoes layered with double cream and freshly grated Parmesan and Gruyère and baked in the oven until creamy and golden); a freshly baked *quiche* filled with a cargo of creamed button onions; a fresh cucumber salad, sprinkled with snippets of fresh tarragon and parsley; and a golden saffron-flavoured *risotto*. All these favourites – easy to make, exciting to serve – you will find in this course. And many more!

You will find, too, that each of the five sections of this Cookery Course is complete in itself with first courses, main courses, vegetable dishes, salads and salad dressings and sweets and puddings. And the selection of recipes in each course is more than ample for planning well-balanced and varied menus for every occasion.

More than a cook book

The whole Cookery Course – book by book, Lesson by Lesson – is full of helpful hints and professional know-how. It is a step-by-step course in cookery which takes you progressively through all the culinary techniques that you need to become a really superb cook, and as you master section after section of the Course, learning progressively all the techniques of gourmet cookery, you will be able to choose your favourite dishes from the whole book to make many memorable meals that will astound your friends and delight yourself.

It was André Simon, I think, who first compared good cooks with great actors. 'They both need,' he confided, 'to be fit and strong, for acting and cooking are two of the most exacting professions in the world. And they should also be blessed with artistic temperament for they need recognition from their audience to make sure they are giving of their best.'

I know that I, for one, really enjoy cooking for guests that appreciate good food and say so. In the old days it used to be considered impolite to even mention the food that had been so painstakingly prepared. Those days are gone forever, thank God, and now we can all sit about the table commenting on the dish that is being served to us, talking about its flavour, its texture, remembering other dishes, other savours; and just plain exuberating in the very fact that we are all together, with old friends and new friends, having the time of our lives.

A way of life

That is what cooking is all about. Giving a dinner party for two, for four, or for more, can be a wonderfully rewarding experience. Yet, so many cooks I know limit themselves to too small a repertoire of favourite recipes. And too many mothers allow themselves to be ruled by their children's lack of interest in trying out new dishes. How many times on my visits around the world have I met women who profess to be 'real gourmets', but who restrict their daily cooking to chops, steaks, or even hamburgers, because 'that's what the children like'.

Every member of the household – from father to the youngest child – should be made to devote a little time to gastronomic exploration and innovation. It's a dull diet indeed if every day, week in and week out, we sit down to the same things, varying this regular monotony perhaps with a few seasonal delicacies – strawberries, asparagus, summer fruits, game – as they first appear … and then falling back into the same old weary routine of daily eating.

We can get so much pleasure and excitement from ringing the changes in our daily menu. The shops are full of possibilities well within our reach, both gastronomically and economically. So, don't get into a food rut. Whether you are feeding the family or special guests, just one or two new dishes a week will make a dramatic difference to your culinary vocabulary and will give them at the same time the pleasure of voting on your latest creations.

It is the small daily variations in our meals that instil new life and interest: a new sauce or garnish for a favourite vegetable; different dressings for various salad combinations; or finding new ways of preparing potatoes, carrots, or Brussels sprouts. So follow the Cookery Course – Lesson by Lesson – and you will soon be a superb cook ready to delight your friends and loved ones with your culinary expertise.

Happy cooking!
Robert Carrier

A short guide to culinary terms

Abaisse French pastry-making term to describe a sheet (or layer) of pastry rolled out to a certain thickness.

Abatis Heart, liver, gizzard, neck and wing tips of fowl.

A la In the manner of. **A l'Allemande** German style. Often means garnished with sauerkraut, sausages or noodles. **A l'Alsacienne** Alsatian style. Usually garnished with sauerkraut and sausages; sometimes with *foie gras*. **A l'Americaine** Usually dressed with a sauce containing tomatoes, dry white wine and brandy. Sometimes means dishes cooked in American style. **A l'Andalouse** Usually dresses fish, poultry and meat dishes with *aubergines*, peppers and tomatoes. **A l'Aurore** Usually garnished with a rose-coloured sauce. **A la Barigoule** Usually contains artichokes, mushrooms and a brown sauce. **A la Bordelaise** Bordeaux style. A rich wine sauce. **A la Bourguignonne** Burgundy style. With button mushrooms, button onions and a rich wine sauce. **A la Crème** Served with cream or cooked in a cream sauce. **A l'Espagnole** Spanish style. With tomatoes and peppers. **A la Financière** With truffles and Madeira sauce. **A la Flamande** Flemish style. Usually with chicory. **A l'Indienne** Indian style. With curry. **A l'Italienne** Italian style. With pasta or with a rich brown sauce garnished with tomatoes, mushrooms and garlic. **A la Jardinière** Gardener's style. With mixed cooked vegetables. **A la Normande** Norman style. With a fish-flavoured *velouté* sauce garnished with mussels, shrimps, etc. Or with apples. **A la Paysanne** Country style. **A la Polonaise** Polish style. With buttered breadcrumbs, finely chopped parsley and hard-boiled eggs. **A la Portugaise** Portuguese style. With tomatoes, onions or garlic. **A la Provençale** Provençal style. With tomatoes, garlic and olive oil.

A la broche Roasted slowly on a revolving spit.

Acidify To add lemon juice or vinegar to a sauce or cooked dish.

Acidulated water (1) Water mixed with an acidifying agent – lemon juice or vinegar – used to blanch sweetbreads, veal or chicken. (2) Lemon juice and water in equal quantities added to sliced apples, pears or bananas to stop them turning brown.

Aiguillette Thin, vertically cut strips of prime cuts of meat. Usually cut from breasts of poultry or game.

Appetiser A small portion of food or drink served before – or for the first course of – a meal.

Aspic The culinary name for calf's foot jelly, or jelly made with bones of meat, fish or poultry. Any meat, fish, poultry, game or vegetable may be served 'in aspic'.

Bain-marie A French kitchen utensil designed to keep liquids at simmering point without coming to the boil. It consists of a saucepan standing in a large pan which is filled with boiling water. A *bain-marie* is a great help in keeping sauces, stews and soups hot without over-cooking. In domestic kitchens, a double saucepan can do double duty as a *bain-marie*.

Bake To cook in dry heat in the oven. This term is usually used only for breads, cakes, cookies, biscuits, pies, tarts and pastries. When meats are cooked in the oven, the term used is 'to roast'.

To bake blind To bake a pastry shell without a filling. To keep the sides of pastry shells from collapsing and the bottom from puffing up during baking, place a piece of aluminium foil or wax paper in the bottom of the pastry case and weight this with dried beans or rice (or a combination of the two). When pastry shells have been baked according to recipe directions, the foil or paper is removed and the beans and rice are returned to a storage jar to be used again and again.

Barbecue To cook meat, poultry, game or fish in the open on a grill or spit over charcoal. Originally this term meant cooking a whole animal over an open fire, or in a pit. Barbecued foods are usually basted with a highly-seasoned sauce during cooking time.

Bard To cover meat, poultry, game (and sometimes fish) with thin strips of pork fat or green bacon before roasting or braising.

Baste To pour or spoon liquid over food as it cooks to moisten and flavour it.

Batter Something that is beaten. Usually means the mixture from which pancakes, pudding and cakes are made. The batter used for pancakes and for coating purposes is made of eggs, flour and milk (or sometimes water) and is fairly liquid in consistency.

Beat To mix with a spoon, spatula, whisk, rotary beater or electric blender; to make a mixture smooth and light by enclosing air.

Beurre manié Equal quantities of butter and flour kneaded together and added bit by bit to a stew, casserole or sauce to thicken it.

Bind To thicken soups or sauces with eggs, cream, etc.

Bisque A rich cream soup made of puréed fish or shellfish.

Blanch To pre-heat in boiling water or steam. This can be done for several reasons: (1) to loosen outer skins of fruits, nuts or vegetables; (2) to whiten sweetbreads, veal or chicken; (3) to remove excess salt or bitter flavour from bacon, gammon, ham, Brussels sprouts, turnips, endive, etc.; (4) to prepare fruits and vegetables for canning, freezing or preserving.

Blend To mix two or more ingredients thoroughly.

Boil To cook in any liquid – usually water, wine or stock or a combination of the three – brought to boiling point and kept there.

Boiling point The temperature at which bubbles rise continually and break over the entire surface of a liquid.

Bone To remove the bones from fish, chicken, poultry or game.

Bouillon A clear soup, broth or stock made with beef, veal or poultry and vegetables. Strained before using.

Bouquet garni A bunch or 'faggot' of culinary herbs. Used to flavour stews, casseroles, sauces. A bouquet garni can be small, medium or large, according to the flavour required for the dish and, of course, according to what the cook has at hand.

Bread To roll in or coat with breadcrumbs before cooking.

Brochette See skewer.

Broil See grill.

Brunoise Finely diced vegetables – carrots, celery, onions, leeks (and sometimes, turnips) – simmered in butter and stock until soft. Used to flavour soups, stuffings, sauces and certain dishes of fish and shellfish.

Caramelise To melt sugar in a thick-bottomed saucepan, stirring continuously, until it is a golden-brown syrup.

Chaud-froid A jellied white sauce made of butter, flour, chicken stock, egg yolks, cream and gelatine. Used to give a handsome shiny white glaze to chicken, ham, etc. Brown *chaud-froid* sauce is used to glaze meat and game.

Chill To place in refrigerator or other cold place until cold.

Chop To cut into very small pieces with a sharp knife or a chopper.

Chowder A fish, clam or oyster stew.

Clarify (1) To clear a stock or broth by adding slightly beaten egg whites and crushed egg shells and bringing liquid to the boil. The stock is then cooled and strained before using. (2) To clarify butter: melt butter and pour off clear liquid, leaving sediment behind.

Coat To dust or roll in flour until surface is covered before cooking.

Cocotte (1) A round or oval casserole with a cover. Usually made of iron or enamelled iron. (2) Individual heatproof dishes used for baking eggs. Usually of earthenware or heatproof china.

Cool To allow to stand at room temperature until no longer warm to the touch. (Not to put in the refrigerator.)

Court-bouillon The liquid in which fish, poultry or meat is cooked to give added flavour. A simple *court-bouillon* consists of water to which you have added 1 bay leaf, 2 stalks celery, 1 Spanish onion, 2 carrots and salt and freshly ground black pepper, to taste. Other additives: wine, vinegar, stock, olive oil, garlic, shallots, cloves, etc.

Cream To work one or more foods with a heavy spoon or a firm spatula until the mixture is soft and creamy. To cream butter and sugar; beat softened butter with electric mixer (or rub against sides of bowl with a wooden spoon) until smooth and fluffy. Gradually beat or rub in sugar until thoroughly blended.

Croûte The pastry case for *pâtés*, e.g. *pâté en croûte*. Usually a brioche, a rich brioche dough or a hot water crust.

Croûton Bread trimmed of crusts, cut to shape (triangles, hearts, dice), rubbed with garlic (optional) and sautéed in oil or butter.

Cut in To combine fat and dry ingredients with two knives, scissor-fashion, or with a pastry blender. When making pastry.

Deep-fry To cook in deep hot fat until crisp and golden. Also known as French-fry.

Devil (1) To grill food with a mixture of butter, mustard, chutney or Worcestershire sauce and fresh breadcrumbs. (2) To cook or serve with a hot 'devil' sauce.

Dice To cut into small even cubes.

Disjoint To cut poultry, game or small animals into serving pieces by dividing at the joint.

Dissolve To mix a dry ingredient with liquid until it is absorbed.

Dredge To coat with flour (or other fine-particled substance) by dusting, sprinkling, or rolling the food in flour, cornflour, cornmeal, sugar, etc.

Dust To sift or sprinkle lightly with a fine-particled substance such as flour, sugar or seasonings.

Duxelles Finely-chopped mushrooms and onion (or shallots), sautéed in butter until soft. Mixture should be quite dry. Used to flavour poached fish and shellfish; dress a fillet of beef or leg of baby lamb before it is wrapped in pastry; or garnish a *papillote*.

Fillet (1) Special cut of beef, lamb, pork or veal; breast of poultry and game; fish cut off the bone lengthwise. (2) To cut any of the above to use in cooking.

Fish fumet A highly concentrated fish stock, made by reducing well-flavoured fish stock. Used to poach fish, fish fillets or fish steaks. Corresponds to essence for meats.

Flake To break into small pieces with a fork.

Flame To pour or spoon alcohol over a dish and ignite it.

Fold in When a mixture has been beaten until light and fluffy, other ingredients must be 'folded' in very gently with a spatula so that the air will not be lost. Blend in new ingredients little by little, turning mixture very gently. Continue only until the ingredients are evenly blended.

Fricassée To cook chicken or veal in fat until golden, and then in a sauce. *Fricassée* is in fact a form of braising.

Fry To cook in a little fat or oil in a frying-pan.

Garniture The garnish or trimming added to a cooked dish (or served at the same time on a separate dish); vegetables, rice, pasta, pastry shapes, *croûtons*, etc.

Glaze A thin coating of syrup or aspic – sometimes coloured with caramel – which is brushed over sweets, puddings, fruits (syrup) or cooked ham, tongue, chicken, beef, pork, veal, etc. (aspic). Food must be cold and quite dry before aspic will set.

Grate To reduce to small particles with a grater.

Gratin To cook '*au gratin*' is to brown food in the oven – usually covered in a sauce and dotted with breadcrumbs, cheese and butter – until a crisp, golden coating forms. A '*gratin*' dish is the heatproof dish used for cooking *au gratin*. Usually oval-shaped, in earthenware or enamelled iron.

Grease To rub lightly with butter, margarine, oil or fat.

Grill To cook by direct heat such as an open fire. In our day, by charcoal, gas or electricity.

Julienne To cut into fine strips the length of a matchstick.

Knead To work dough with hands until it is of the desired elasticity or consistency.

Lard (1) Common cooking fat obtained by melting down of pork fat. (2) Culinary process by which lardons of pork fat or green bacon are threaded through meat, poultry, game (and sometimes fish) to lend flavour and moisture to food.

Lardons (1) Strips of fat or green bacon used as above. (2) Diced pork fat or green bacon, blanched and sautéed to add flavour and texture contrast to certain stews, *daubes*, *ragoûts* and casseroles.

Liaison To thicken a sauce, gravy or stew: (1) by the addition of flour, cornflour, arrowroot, rice flour, potato flour, or a *beurre manié* (flour and butter); (2) by stirring in egg yolk, double cream, or in the case of certain dishes of poultry or game, blood.

Macédoine (1) A mixture of raw or cooked fruit for a fruit salad. (2) A mixture of cooked diced vegetables garnished with a cream sauce, mayonnaise or aspic, usually served as an *hors-d'œuvre* salad, or as a garnish.

Marinade A highly flavoured liquid – usually red or white wine or olive oil or a combination of the two – seasoned with carrots, onion, bay leaf, herbs and spices. Marinades can be cooked or uncooked. The purpose of a marinade is to impart flavour to the food and to soften fibres of tougher foods.

Marinate To let food stand, or steep, in a marinade. See above.

Mask To cover cooked food with sauce.

Mince To reduce to very small particles with a mincer, chopper or knife.

Mirepoix Finely–diced carrots, onion, celery (and sometimes ham), simmered in butter until soft. Used to add flavour to dishes of meat, poultry, fish and shellfish.

Oven-fry To cook meat, fish or poultry in fat in the oven, uncovered, basting food with fat from time to time.

Panade A mixture of soft breadcrumbs, egg yolk (and sometimes cream).

Pommade A thick, smooth paste.

Parboil To pre-cook, or boil until partially cooked.

Pare or Peel (1) To cut off outside skin or covering of a fruit or vegetable with a knife or parer. (2) To peel fruits such as oranges or bananas without using a knife.

Papillote To cook '*en papillote*' is the culinary term for cooking food enclosed in an oiled paper or foil case (*papillote*).

Poach To cook gently in simmering (not boiling) liquid so that the surface of the liquid barely trembles.

Pit To remove pit, stone or seed, as from cherries.

Pound To reduce to very small particles, or a paste, with a mortar and pestle.

Purée To press through a fine sieve or food mill to produce a smooth, soft food.

Quenelle The finely-pounded flesh of fish, shellfish, veal, poultry or game; mixed with egg whites and cream and pounded over ice to a velvety smooth paste. These feather-light dumplings are then poached in a light stock or salted water.

Ragoût A stew made from regular-sized pieces of meat, poultry or fish sautéed in fat until brown and then simmered with stock, meat juices or water, or a combination of these, until tender. *Navarin de mouton* is an example of a 'brown' *ragoût* (Irish stew is a typical 'white' *ragoût* in which meat is not browned before stewing).

Ramekin A small, earthenware dish for cooking individual portions: eggs, vegetables and seafood *gratin*, etc.

Reduce To cook a sauce over a high heat, uncovered, until it is reduced by evaporation to the desired consistency. This culinary process improves both flavour and appearance.

Render To free fat from tissue by melting at low heat.

Roast To cook meat by direct heat on a spit or in the oven; although 'baking' would be a better term in the latter case, for when meat is cooked in a closed area (oven) vapour accumulates and changes texture and flavour of true roast.

Roux The gentle amalgamation of butter and flour over a low heat; capable of absorbing at least six times its own weight when cooked. (1) To make a white *roux*: melt 2 tablespoons butter in the top of a double saucepan; add 2 tablespoons of sieved flour and stir with a wire whisk for two to three minutes over water until the mixture amalgamates but does not change colour. (2) A pale *roux*: cook as above stirring continuously, just a little longer (four to five minutes) or until the colour of the *roux* begins to change to pale gold. (3) A brown *roux*: cook as before until mixture acquires a fine, light-brown colour and nutty aroma.

Salmis To cook jointed poultry or game in a rich wine sauce after it has been roasted until almost done. Often done in a chafing dish at the table.

Salpicon Finely diced meat, poultry, game, fish, shellfish or vegetables, bound with a savoury sauce and used to fill *canapés* and individual *hors-d'œuvre* pastry cases. Also used to make *rissoles*, *croquettes* and stuffings for eggs, vegetables and small cuts of poultry or meat.

Sauté To fry lightly in a small amount of hot fat or oil, shaking the pan or turning food frequently during cooking.

Scald To heat to temperature just below boiling point. I use a double saucepan to scald cream or milk. This prevents scorching.

Score To make evenly spaced, shallow slits or cuts with a knife.

Sear To brown and seal the surface of meat quickly over high heat. This prevents juices from escaping.

Sift To put through a sifter or a fine sieve.

Simmer To cook in liquid just below boiling point, with small bubbles of steam rising gently to the surface.

Skewer (1) To keep in shape with skewers. (2) The actual 'skewer' – made of metal or wood – which is used to keep meats, poultry, game, etc., in shape while cooking. (3) The 'skewer' – piece of metal or wood – sometimes called 'brochette' used to hold pieces of chicken, fish, poultry, etc., to be grilled over charcoal, or under gas or electricity.

Sliver To cut or shred into long, thin pieces.

Steam To cook food in vapour over boiling water. This process is often used in Oriental cooking.

Steep To let food stand in hot liquid to extract flavour or colour.

Stir To mix with a spoon or fork with a circular motion until ingredients are well blended.

Whisk To beat rapidly with a whisk, rotary beater or electric mixer in order to incorporate air and increase volume.

Zest The finely grated rind of lemon or orange.

How to follow a recipe successfully

Read the recipe carefully through to the end. Calculate *total* preparation time, including hold-ups while marinating, chilling, etc. Make sure that you have all the necessary ingredients and utensils before you begin the recipe; and that all utensils are of the correct size.

Assemble ingredients and utensils *before* you start. Remove eggs, butter, meat, etc., from refrigerator in advance so that they will be at room temperature by the time you start to cook.

Do any advance preparation indicated in list of ingredients. The preparation of cake tins, etc., should also be attended to before you start.

Measure or weigh ingredients carefully.

Do not be tempted to alter a recipe in mid-stream until you have prepared it faithfully at least once, and do not telescope or ignore directions and procedures for combining ingredients unless you are a very experienced cook.

Follow cooking and/or baking times and temperature given, but test for doneness about two-thirds of the way through or, conversely, be prepared to increase cooking time if it appears insufficient. Oven heats can vary considerably.

How to measure correctly

All spoon measurements in this book are level.

Accurate measurement is essential to any kind of cooking. A standard set of individual measuring spoons in plastic or metal – 1 tablespoon, 1 teaspoon, $\frac{1}{2}$ teaspoon and $\frac{1}{4}$ teaspoon – is ideal for small quantities and can be bought in many kitchen departments throughout the country. When a recipe calls for a fraction not catered for in the standard set, a dry ingredient can be measured by taking a whole spoonful, then carefully halving or quartering the amount with the tip of a knife and discarding the excess.

Larger quantities

For measuring larger quantities of ingredients you will also need:

A measuring jug marked off in fluid ounces and heatproof to withstand boiling liquids. You will also find this useful to use with American recipes, but remember the American pint measures only 16 fluid ounces, and the American cup (or $\frac{1}{2}$ pint) measures 8 fluid ounces.

Kitchen scales Select a pair with a large enough pan to hold the quantities you are likely to be measuring. You should be able to measure a pound of flour without spilling.

Metrication

The exact conversion from Imperial to metric measures does not
usually give very convenient working quantities and so for greater
convenience we have rounded off metric measures into units of
twenty-five grammes. The table below shows recommended
equivalents.

Ounces/fluid ounces	Approximate g and ml to nearest whole figure	Recommended conversion to nearest unit of 25
1	28	25
2	57	50
3	85	75
4	113	100
5 ($\frac{1}{4}$ pint)	142	150
6	170	175
7	198	200
8 ($\frac{1}{2}$lb)	226	225
9	255	250
10 ($\frac{1}{2}$ pint)	283	275
11	311	300
12	340	350
13	368	375
14	396	400
15 ($\frac{3}{4}$ pint)	428	425
16 (1lb)	456	450
17	484	475
18	512	500
19	541	550
20 (1 pint)	569	575

When converting quantities over 20oz first add the appropriate
figures in the centre column, *then* adjust to the nearest unit of
twenty-five. As a general guide, 1kg (1000g) equals 2.2lb or about
2lb 3oz, 1 litre (1000ml) equals 1.76 pints or almost exactly 1$\frac{3}{4}$ pints.

This method of conversion gives good results in nearly all recipes. However, where the proportion between liquids and solids is critical, for example in baking recipes, a more accurate conversion is necessary to preserve the exact proportions of the recipe. In these cases use a conversion to the nearest five grammes; for example, 4oz should be converted to 110g instead of 100g in the chart, to give a more exact quantity.

Can sizes Because at present cans are marked with the exact (usually to the nearest whole number) metric equivalent of the Imperial weight of the contents, we have followed this practice when giving can sizes. Thus the equivalent of a 14oz can of tomatoes would be a 396g can, and not 400g which is the usual recommended conversion when you are measuring your own ingredients.

Oven temperatures

The chart below gives the Celsius (Centigrade) equivalents recommended in this book.

Description	Fahrenheit	Celsius	Gas mark
Cool	225	110	$\frac{1}{4}$
	250	130	$\frac{1}{2}$
Very slow	275	140	1
	300	150	2
Slow	325	170	3
Moderate	350	180	4
	375	190	5
Moderately hot	400	200	6
Fairly hot	425	220	7
Hot	450	230	8
Very hot	475	240	9
Extremely hot	500	250	10

Liquid measures The millilitre is a very small unit of measurement and we feel that to use decilitres (units of 100ml) is less cumbersome. In most cases it is perfectly satisfactory to round off the exact millilitre conversion to the nearest decilitre, except for $\frac{1}{4}$ pint: thus $\frac{1}{4}$ pint (142ml) is $1\frac{1}{2}$dl, $\frac{1}{2}$ pint (283ml) is 3dl, $\frac{3}{4}$ pint (428ml) is 4dl, and 1 pint (569ml) is 6dl. For quantities over 1 pint, use litres and fractions of a litre, using the conversion rate of $1\frac{3}{4}$ pints to 1 litre.

First course salads and vegetables

When making first course salads and vegetable appetisers, bear the following important points in mind:

* An appetiser salad or vegetable dish is designed to stimulate the appetite without satisfying it.

* It must be attractive to the eye as well as the palate – this is the first impression your guests will get of the meal you have prepared for them, and we all know how first impressions linger the longest.

* Make a point of using the finest, fruitiest olive oil, a mellow wine vinegar, freshly ground black peppercorns and a good, coarse salt when you come to dress a salad, prepare a mayonnaise or simmer vegetables for a cold antipasto or a dish à la Grecque.

* Finally, remember that just as a salad ought to be crisp, so cooked vegetables must never be taken beyond the stage where textures break down to a uniform, lifeless mush. They should be neither raw, nor overcooked, but *al dente* – the stage at which texture and, as a result, flavour are at their peak.

Belgian appetiser salad

Serves 4
¾lb green beans
¾lb new potatoes
Salt
2 level tablespoons butter
8–10oz streaky bacon, cut in strips
1 Spanish onion, finely chopped

4 tablespoons wine vinegar
Freshly ground black pepper
2 level tablespoons finely chopped parsley

1 Trim and wash beans. Wash potatoes without peeling them. Boil
beans and potatoes until tender in separate pans of salted water,
twelve to fifteen minutes for the beans, and about twenty-five
minutes for the potatoes.

2 In the meantime, melt butter in a deep frying-pan or sauté dish
and sauté bacon strips until crisp and golden, about five minutes.

3 Add finely chopped onion and sauté until soft but not coloured.

4 Sprinkle with wine vinegar and heat gently for a further three
minutes. Keep hot.

5 When beans are tender, drain them thoroughly and place them in a
salad bowl.

6 Drain potatoes; peel them and cut into $\frac{1}{4}$in thick slices. Add them
to the beans and season lightly with salt and freshly ground black
pepper.

7 Pour bacon mixture over hot beans and potatoes, and toss gently
until well mixed. Serve lukewarm, sprinkled with finely chopped
parsley.

Provençal cauliflower salad

Serves 6
2 medium-sized cauliflowers
Salt
6 anchovy fillets, finely chopped
12 black olives, pitted and chopped
3 level tablespoons finely chopped parsley
1 clove garlic, finely chopped
1 level tablespoon finely chopped capers
6 tablespoons olive oil
2 tablespoons wine vinegar
Freshly ground black pepper

1 Trim cauliflowers and cut out any bruised spots. Break into flowerets; rinse well and poach gently in lightly salted water for about five minute... They should remain crisp and if anything slightly undercooked.

2 Drain flowerets carefully and leave them in a bowl of cold water until ready to use.

3 In a small bowl, combine finely chopped anchovies, black olives, parsley, garlic and capers with olive oil and wine vinegar. Season to taste with salt and freshly ground black pepper.

4 When ready to serve: drain flowerets and dry them carefully in a cloth. Arrange them in a serving dish; spoon anchovy dressing over the top and serve immediately, tossing salad lightly at the table.

Caesar salad

Serves 6
2 cloves garlic
$\frac{1}{4}$ pint olive oil
2 heads Cos lettuce
$\frac{1}{2}$ level teaspoon salt
$\frac{1}{4}$ level teaspoon each dry mustard and freshly ground black pepper
4 tablespoons lemon juice
2 eggs
3–4 slices bread, $\frac{1}{4}$ in thick
4 anchovy fillets, finely chopped (optional)
8 level tablespoons freshly grated Parmesan

1 Peel garlic cloves and crush them lightly in a small bowl. Add the olive oil and leave them to steep for about two hours, so that the oil becomes heavily impregnated with their flavour. Strain oil through a fine sieve, discarding garlic.

2 Wash and drain Cos lettuce, and pat each leaf dry with a clean cloth. (This is important, as any water remaining on the leaves would dilute the dressing.) Break leaves into a salad bowl in fairly large pieces.

3 Combine salt, dry mustard and freshly ground black pepper with lemon juice. Beat in 6 tablespoons of the garlic-flavoured oil to make a vinaigrette dressing.

4 Drop eggs into boiling water; simmer for just ninety seconds and drain immediately. (This is known as 'coddling'.)

5 Cut bread slices into ¼in cubes. Heat remaining garlic oil in a frying pan and sauté bread cubes until crisp and golden brown all over, adding a little more oil if necessary. Drain well on absorbent paper.

6 To assemble salad: toss lettuce with vinaigrette dressing and chopped anchovies, if used. When the leaves are well coated with dressing, break coddled eggs into the centre and toss again. Finally, add garlic croûtons and finely grated Parmesan, and toss lightly but thoroughly until there is no more dressing left at the bottom of the bowl. Serve immediately.

Herbed salad niçoise

Serves 4

1lb small waxy potatoes
Salt
2–3 eggs
¼ Spanish onion, thinly sliced and separated into rings
1 medium-sized green pepper
4 stalks celery
One 7oz can tuna, drained and coarsely flaked
4 large firm tomatoes, peeled
One 2oz can anchovy fillets, drained and sliced in half lengthwise
12 black olives, pitted

Dressing
¼ pint olive oil
2 tablespoons dry white wine
2 tablespoons wine vinegar
½ level teaspoon French mustard
1 shallot, grated

Salt and freshly ground black pepper
1 level tablespoon finely chopped parsley
$\frac{1}{4}$ level teaspoon each dried marjoram, chervil and tarragon

1 Boil potatoes in their jackets in salted water until just tender, fifteen to twenty minutes.

2 Meanwhile, prepare dressing: whisk or beat olive oil, wine, wine vinegar and mustard together until they emulsify. Stir in grated shallot and season to taste with salt and freshly ground black pepper.

3 As soon as potatoes are tender, cool the pan under cold running water until they can just be handled. Peel and slice them into a salad bowl.

4 Pour 4 or 5 tablespoons dressing over hot potato slices. Mix gently and leave to cool.

5 Add herbs to remaining dressing.

6 Boil eggs for ten minutes. Drain, cover with cold water and leave to cool.

7 Soak onion rings in cold water for ten minutes. Drain, pat dry and add to bowl.

8 Halve, core and seed pepper, and slice into thin strips. Add to salad bowl.

9 Slice celery stalks $\frac{1}{2}$in thick. Add to the bowl together with coarsely flaked tuna, and mix thoroughly, taking care not to break potato slices.

10 Halve tomatoes and cut each half into three wedges.

11 Shell and quarter hard-boiled eggs.

12 Arrange tomato wedges, quartered hard-boiled eggs and halved anchovy fillets decoratively on top of salad. Dot with pitted black

olives, halved if they are very large. Spoon over some of the dressing and serve remainder separately.

Russian chicken and potato salad

Serves 4
½ cooked chicken
½lb potatoes, boiled in their jackets
2 large dill pickles
One 7½oz can button mushrooms, drained
2 teaspoons Worcestershire sauce
Salt and freshly ground black pepper
6 black olives, pitted and halved
2 hard-boiled eggs, sliced

Classic mayonnaise

2 egg yolks (at room temperature)
½ level teaspoon English or French mustard
Salt and freshly ground black pepper
Lemon juice
½ pint olive oil

1 Skin and bone chicken, and cut meat into short, thin strips.

2 Peel boiled potatoes and cut them into strips of the same size.

3 Cut dill pickles into matching strips.

4 In a bowl, combine chicken, potatoes and pickles with button mushrooms. Mix lightly, taking care not to break potatoes.

5 Prepare mayonnaise: put egg yolks in a medium-sized bowl and set it in a pan or on a damp cloth on the table to hold it steady. Add mustard and a pinch each of salt and freshly ground black pepper, and work to a smooth paste with a spoon or whisk.

6 Add a teaspoon of lemon juice and work until smooth again. Pour olive oil into a measuring jug. With a teaspoon, start adding oil to egg yolk mixture a drop at a time, beating well between each addition.

7 Having incorporated about a quarter of the oil, step up the rate at which you add the remainder of the oil, a teaspoon or two at a time, or a steady, fine trickle, beating strongly as you do so. If the mayonnaise becomes very thick before all the oil has been absorbed, thin it down again with more lemon juice or a few drops of cold water. Correct seasoning, adding more salt, freshly ground black pepper or lemon juice if necessary.

8 Beat Worcestershire sauce into 6 level tablespoons of the mayonnaise and carefully fold into salad with a large spoon, adding salt and freshly ground black pepper, to taste.

9 Mound salad in a shallow serving dish. Mask with remaining mayonnaise and decorate with pieces of olive and slices of hard-boiled egg.

10 Chill until ready to serve.

German potato salad with bacon

Serves 4, or 6–8 as part of a selection of *hors-d'œuvres*
1½lb small new potatoes
Chicken stock (made with a cube)
3–4 slices bacon
1 medium-sized onion, finely chopped
6 tablespoons olive oil
3 tablespoons cider vinegar
1 level tablespoon sugar
1 teaspoon Worcestershire sauce
2–3 drops Tabasco
Salt and freshly ground black pepper

1 Scrub potatoes clean. Boil them in their jackets in water flavoured with a chicken stock cube until just tender. (If potatoes are large, cut them in half to allow flavour of stock to penetrate.)

2 Meanwhile, dice bacon finely and fry until crisp in a small pan. Put aside.

3 When potatoes are tender, drain and cool them slightly; then peel

37

and dice them (or slice them if they are small enough) and put them in a bowl.

4 To the crisp-fried bacon add finely chopped onion, olive oil, cider vinegar, sugar, Worcestershire sauce and Tabasco. Heat gently, stirring, without allowing mixture to come to the boil.

5 Pour hot dressing over hot potatoes; mix lightly and leave to cool.

6 Season salad to taste with salt and freshly ground black pepper, and chill lightly before serving.

Chick peas rémoulade

Serves 6–8 as part of a selection of *hors-d'œuvre* dishes
½lb chick peas, soaked overnight
1 can anchovy fillets, drained and chopped
1 clove garlic, crushed
2 level tablespoons capers, chopped
1 level tablespoon finely chopped shallots or spring onions
2 level tablespoons finely chopped parsley
¼ pint thick mayonnaise (p.36)
1 level teaspoon French mustard
Salt and freshly ground black pepper
1 tablespoon lemon juice (optional)
Parsley sprigs, to garnish

1 Drain soaked chick peas and cover with fresh water in a saucepan. (Do not salt the water, or chick peas will not soften.) Bring to the boil and simmer until chick peas are tender, about forty-five minutes, depending on their quality and age. Drain and leave until cold.

2 Combine next five ingredients in a bowl.

3 Flavour thick mayonnaise with French mustard. Blend with chopped anchovy mixture.

4 Fold enough of the anchovy-flavoured mayonnaise into chick peas to dress them richly. Any left-over mayonnaise may be served separately in a bowl so that people may help themselves to more if they wish.

5 Season chick peas with salt and freshly ground black pepper, to taste, and a little lemon juice if you like.

6 Garnish with parsley sprigs and chill until ready to serve.

Pois chiches en salade

Serves 4–6 as part of a selection of *hors-d'œuvre* dishes
6oz chick peas, soaked overnight
6 spring onions, finely chopped
2 level tablespoons finely chopped parsley
1 clove garlic, finely chopped
One 3½oz can tuna fish, drained and flaked

Dressing
8 tablespoons olive oil
2 tablespoons wine vinegar
1 tablespoon lemon juice
Salt and freshly ground black pepper

1 Drain soaked chick peas and cook them in a fresh portion of unsalted water until tender, as above.

2 Drain chick peas thoroughly, and while still hot toss in a salad bowl with finely chopped spring onions, parsley and garlic.

3 To make dressing: beat ingredients together with a fork until they form an emulsion, adding salt and freshly ground black pepper, to taste.

4 Pour dressing over chick peas. Add flaked tuna fish and toss together lightly until well mixed.

If you want to serve the salad on its own, use a 7oz can of tuna instead of the smaller size.

Brussels sprout appetiser

Serves 4, or 6–8 as part of a selection of *hors-d'œuvre* dishes
1lb baby sprouts

Salt
$\frac{1}{4}$ pint olive oil
2–3 tablespoons wine vinegar
Generous pinch of dry mustard
Generous pinch of sugar
Freshly ground black pepper
A few lettuce leaves
2 level tablespoons finely chopped onion
4 level tablespoons finely chopped parsley

1 Trim Brussels sprouts, removing overblown or yellowed leaves, and nicking a small cross in the base of each stem so that heat will penetrate and cook them evenly.

2 Bring a pan of salted water to a brisk boil. Drop in Brussels sprouts; bring to the boil again and simmer until just tender, five to seven minutes.

3 Meanwhile, beat olive oil and wine vinegar with a fork, adding mustard, sugar, salt and freshly ground black pepper, to taste.

4 Drain Brussels sprouts thoroughly. Shake them gently in the pan for a few seconds over moderate heat to evaporate any remaining moisture. Put them in a bowl.

5 Pour dressing over hot sprouts. Toss lightly and leave to marinate for an hour or two.

6 To serve: line a salad bowl with lettuce leaves. Pile Brussels sprouts and juices in the centre, and garnish with finely chopped onion and parsley.

French cabbage salad

Serves 4
$\frac{1}{2}$ head firm white or green cabbage (8–10oz)
4 tablespoons olive oil
1 tablespoon lemon juice
2 level tablespoons soured cream
1 clove garlic, crushed

2 level tablespoons castor sugar
Salt and freshly ground black pepper
1 crisp dessert apple, peeled, cored and chopped

1 Shred cabbage very thinly. Soak in cold water for five minutes. Drain thoroughly, pressing out as much moisture as possible.

2 Make a dressing by beating oil and lemon juice with a fork until they form an emulsion. Add soured cream gradually, beating constantly. Flavour dressing with crushed garlic and sugar, and season to taste with salt and freshly ground black pepper.

3 In a serving bowl, toss drained cabbage with freshly chopped apple. Pour over dressing; mix well and chill until ready to serve.

Stuffed cucumber appetiser

Serves 4–6
1 cucumber
Salt
Iced water
One 7oz can tuna fish in oil
3 level tablespoons softened butter
$\frac{1}{4}$ level teaspoon each thyme, oregano, tarragon and chives
2 level teaspoons finely chopped parsley
Freshly ground black pepper
Lettuce leaves, to garnish

1 Trim both ends of cucumber. Peel off skin very thinly and cut cucumber across into three thick chunks. Drop pieces into boiling salted water and simmer for ten minutes. Drain thoroughly; then soak in iced water for ten minutes to firm them.

2 Carefully scoop out seeds from each piece of cucumber to leave a ring $\frac{2}{3}$in thick. Leave to drain while you prepare filling.

3 Pound well–drained tuna fish to a paste with butter. Add herbs; mix well and season to taste with salt and freshly ground black pepper.

4 Fill cucumber rings tightly with tuna fish paste and chill in refrigerator until firm.

5 Serve chilled cucumber cut in thin slices and arranged on a bed of
   lettuce leaves.

Italian pepper appetiser

Serves 6
8 sweet peppers
6–8 anchovy fillets
3 cloves garlic, finely chopped
3 level tablespoons finely chopped parsley
4 tablespoons olive oil
2 teaspoons lemon juice
Salt and freshly ground black pepper (optional)

1 Place peppers side by side in a grill–pan and grill steadily under a
   moderate heat until their skins blister and blacken all over, and
   peppers become rather limp. Keep turning them so that every part
   is exposed to the heat.

2 Plunge grilled peppers into a large bowl of cold water. Leave them
   for two minutes; then drain and peel. Skins will slip off quite
   easily if peppers have been correctly and evenly grilled. Slice
   peppers in half; cut out pith and rinse out seeds under cold running
   water. Pat each piece of pepper dry and cut it in four across the
   width.

3 Cut anchovy fillets into $\frac{1}{4}$ in lengths and combine them in a deep
   serving dish with peppers and finely chopped garlic and parsley.
   Toss lightly until well mixed.

4 Heat olive oil with lemon juice in a small pan. When it is very hot,
   pour it all over the peppers and mix lightly. Leave to become quite
   cold – the dressing helps to develop and blend flavours together as
   it cools in a way that a simple cold dressing could never do. Serve
   chilled.

Note: This dish is so strongly flavoured that you are unlikely to
need either salt or pepper, but taste and judge for yourself.

Potato and tongue salad

Serves 6
2lb firm salad potatoes
Salt
3–4 tablespoons dry white wine
2 tablespoons tarragon vinegar
Freshly ground black pepper
8–12oz cooked tongue, sliced $\frac{3}{8}$in thick
$\frac{1}{2}$ pint thick lemon mayonnaise (p.36)
2 level tablespoons finely chopped parsley
1–2 level teaspoons tarragon (see Note)
2–3 crisp dessert apples
Lettuce leaves and chopped parsley, to garnish

1 Scrub potatoes thoroughly and boil them in salted water until just soft. Cover with cold water until cool enough to handle; then peel carefully and cut into small, chip-like strips. Place in a large bowl.

2 While potatoes are still warm, sprinkle with a mixture of white wine and tarragon vinegar; toss lightly and season to taste with salt and freshly ground black pepper.

3 Cut sliced tongue into strips of the same size. Mix carefully with warm potatoes and leave until quite cold.

4 Meanwhile, prepare a well-seasoned lemon mayonnaise. Add finely chopped parsley and tarragon, to taste.

5 Peel, core and dice apples, folding pieces into the bowl of mayonnaise as soon as you have cut them to prevent discolouration.

6 Combine potato-tongue mixture with apple mayonnaise. Taste and add more salt or freshly ground black pepper if necessary.

7 Serve cold but not chilled in a lettuce-lined bowl, dusted with more chopped parsley.

Note: When fresh tarragon is not available, use $\frac{1}{2}$–1 level teaspoon dried tarragon 'infused' for ten minutes in boiling water and drained on a sheet of absorbent paper.

Almond chicken salad

Serves 4
½lb cooked chicken, diced
4 stalks celery, thinly sliced
2oz flaked almonds, toasted
2 level tablespoons very finely chopped onion
1 tablespoon lemon juice
¼ pint thick home-made mayonnaise (p.36)
4 level tablespoons double cream, lightly whipped
Tabasco
Salt and freshly ground black pepper
Lettuce leaves, to garnish

1 Combine chicken with celery and half the almonds in a large bowl.

2 In another bowl, mix very finely chopped onion with lemon juice,
  mayonnaise, lightly whipped cream and a dash of Tabasco. Add
  to chicken and celery, and toss until well coated with dressing.

3 Season salad to taste with salt and freshly ground black pepper, and
  chill until ready to serve.

4 To serve: line four individual serving dishes with lettuce leaves.
  Divide salad between them and decorate with remaining toasted
  almonds.

Curried rice salad

Serves 6–8

Mayonnaise aspic mould
½ pint thick home-made mayonnaise (p.36)
2 level teaspoons curry paste
2 teaspoons lemon juice
One 3½oz can tuna fish
1 large green pepper
1 large red pepper
½ pint liquid aspic
Salt and freshly ground black pepper

Rice salad
8oz long-grain rice, cooked and drained
One 7oz can tuna fish, coarsely flaked
8oz white button mushrooms
Juice of $\frac{1}{2}$ large lemon
2 level tablespoons finely chopped parsley
6 tablespoons olive oil
3 tablespoons wine vinegar
$\frac{1}{2}$ level teaspoon curry paste
Salt and freshly ground black pepper

Garnish
1 small pepper, multi-coloured if possible

A creamy mayonnaise aspic with a faint flavour of curry, served with a light rice salad spiked with crisp pieces of sweet pepper. Use curry paste if you can get it, as uncooked curry powder tends to leave a crude aftertaste.

1 Prepare *mayonnaise aspic mould:* in a large bowl, blend mayonnaise thoroughly with curry paste and flavour with lemon juice.

2 Turn contents of can of tuna fish into a small bowl and work to a paste with a fork – alternatively, purée at moderate speed for thirty seconds in an electric blender. Add to the curried mayonnaise and mix well.

3 Cut both green and red peppers in half; remove cores, seeds and stems, then slice green pepper into thin strips and the red one into small dice. Add half of each pepper to the mayonnaise, and reserve remainder for the salad.

4 When aspic is on the point of setting, stir into mayonnaise gently, to avoid creating air bubbles. Season generously with salt and freshly ground black pepper.

5 Lightly oil a plain, 2 pint ring mould (choose one with a wide hole in the centre, into which you can later pile the rice salad). Pour in mayonnaise aspic and chill in the refrigerator for one and a half to two hours, until firmly set.

6 Meanwhile, prepare *rice salad:* turn cooked rice into a large bowl. Add flaked tuna fish and remaining green and red peppers, and mix lightly.

7 Slice button mushrooms thinly and toss with lemon juice to prevent discolouration. Add them to the rice mixture, together with finely chopped parsley, and toss again.

8 Make a dressing for the salad with olive oil, wine vinegar, curry paste, and salt and freshly ground black pepper, to taste. Pour over salad; give it a final good toss and taste for seasoning, adding more salt or freshly ground black pepper if necessary. Chill until ready to serve.

9 Just before serving: turn ring mould out in the centre of a large flat dish. (Do this by turning the mould upside down on the dish, wrapping a cloth wrung out of hot water round the top and sides for a few seconds, then shaking the mould gently until it comes loose. You may have to use the hot cloth several times, but do not leave it for more than a few seconds each time, or the surface of the mayonnaise aspic will start to melt.)

10 Heap the rice salad in the centre of the mould. Core and seed remaining pepper; cut it into thin strips, and use it to decorate top of ring mould and salad. Serve any left-over rice salad in a separate bowl.

Cauliflower à la Grecque

Serves 4–6
1 cauliflower, about 2lb
8–10 tablespoons olive oil
2 carrots, finely diced
1 Spanish onion, finely chopped
¼ pint dry white wine
12 black peppercorns, lightly crushed
Bouquet garni
1 fat clove garlic
18 coriander seeds
½lb tomatoes, peeled and seeded

Salt
Lemon juice
2 level tablespoons finely chopped parsley
8–12 black olives, pitted

1 Wash cauliflower and break into flowerets of roughly the same size. Put aside.

2 Heat 4 tablespoons olive oil in a heavy saucepan or flameproof casserole and sauté carrots and onion over a moderate heat for five minutes until golden.

3 Remove pan from heat. Add white wine, lightly crushed peppercorns, bouquet garni, garlic clove, coriander seeds and peeled, seeded tomatoes. Mix well; then add pieces of cauliflower, turning them over carefully to coat them thoroughly with the sauce.

4 Season to taste with salt and cook over a moderate heat for fifteen to twenty minutes, or until cauliflower is tender but still on the crisp side, stirring occasionally and adding a little more wine (or water) if sauce evaporates too quickly. Sauce should be rather scarce by the time the cauliflower is cooked. Remove from heat and allow to cool.

5 When mixture is cold, remove bouquet garni and garlic clove. Stir in remaining olive oil. Correct seasoning if necessary and add a little lemon juice to bring out flavours.

6 Arrange cauliflower in a serving dish. Garnish with finely chopped parsley; dot with black olives and chill lightly until ready to serve.

Courgettes à la Grecque

Serves 4–6
6 tablespoons olive oil
1 large Spanish onion, finely chopped
1 large clove garlic, finely chopped
$\frac{1}{4}$ pint dry white wine
Bouquet garni
12 coriander seeds

12 black peppercorns
Lemon juice
Salt
1½lb small sweet courgettes
2–4 level tablespoons finely chopped parsley

1 Heat 4 tablespoons olive oil in a heavy pan or casserole; add finely
  chopped onion and garlic, and sauté until transparent. Add wine,
  ¼ pint water, bouquet garni, coriander seeds, black peppercorns,
  the juice of 1 lemon, and salt, to taste. Bring to the boil and simmer
  gently for five minutes.

2 Wipe courgettes with a damp cloth. Trim ends; quarter courgettes
  and cut them into 2in segments (they should not be peeled). Add
  courgettes to simmering sauce and cook over a low heat for twenty
  to twenty-five minutes, or until tender but still firm.

3 Transfer courgettes to a deep serving dish, discarding bouquet
  garni. Pour over cooking juices and allow to cool. Then chill until
  ready to serve.

4 Just before serving, moisten with remaining olive oil. Sprinkle
  with the finely chopped parsley and a little lemon juice, to taste,
  and serve immediately.

Onions à la Grecque

Serves 4
2lb button onions
¼–½ pint dry white wine
5oz sugar
5oz plumped-up raisins
4 level tablespoons tomato concentrate
4 tablespoons olive oil
2–4 tablespoons wine vinegar
Salt and freshly ground black pepper
Cayenne pepper
Coarsely chopped parsley

1 Peel onions.

2 Combine in a saucepan with 1 pint water, the dry white wine, sugar, plumped-up raisins, tomato concentrate and olive oil. Add wine vinegar, salt, freshly ground black pepper and cayenne pepper, to taste, and simmer for about forty-five minutes, or until onions are tender, but still quite firm.

3 Serve cold, garnished with coarsely chopped parsley.

Artichoke hearts à la Grecque

Serves 6
6 tender artichokes
Juice of 1–2 lemons
6oz onion, minced or grated
12 button onions
Salt
6–8 tablespoons olive oil
Freshly ground black pepper

Only the hearts of the artichokes are used in this dish. Boil the leaves separately in salted, acidulated water until tender, and serve them with a bowl of melted butter or vinaigrette to dip into. They are far too good to waste.

1 To prepare artichokes: lay each artichoke on its side and slice off the leaves level with the choke. Then, holding the artichoke firmly, peel round with a sharp knife from the base to remove remaining leaves right down to the heart. Have ready a bowl of cold water heavily acidulated with lemon juice and immerse the artichoke in it as soon as you have cut down to the heart. Otherwise it quickly goes black when exposed to the air.

2 Now scrape out all the fibres or 'choke' growing on the heart, dipping it into the bowl of lemon water occasionally to keep it white.

3 Prepare remaining artichoke hearts in the same way.

4 Arrange artichoke hearts side by side in one layer in a wide, shallow pan. Spoon some of the minced or grated onion over each one.

5 Slip button onions in between hearts and barely cover with salted water.

6 Bring to the boil; cover pan and simmer gently until artichoke hearts and onions are tender, about twenty minutes. Then remove lid; pour in olive oil and raise heat under the pan. Boil hard for about ten minutes, or until water has evaporated, leaving the oil behind.

7 Transfer artichoke hearts and button onions to a shallow serving dish, spooning pan juices over them. Season to taste with freshly ground black pepper and more salt if necessary. Sprinkle with a little lemon juice and chill until ready to serve.

Note: If you feel the dish is too dry, you can spoon over a little more raw olive oil just before serving.

Pancakes

The pancake

Take the cooking of any country and you are practically certain to come across a pancake in one guise or another. Indeed, pancakes may well have been the earliest form of bread – finely ground grain mixed with water, formed into flat cakes and baked on hot stones – before the discovery of leavening agents, and they still are in some parts of the world.

Large or small, fat or thin, stuffed or plain, and made with every conceivable type of flour, from robust maize and buckwheat to the silkiest white wheat, pancakes come under a variety of names: German pfannkuchen and palatschinken, Russian bliny, Jewish blintzes and latkes (potato pancakes), Spanish–Mexican tortillas, Swedish plättar, Norwegian lefser, even, at a pinch, the Indian paratha, but the most famous of them all is the great French crêpe.

Once you have learned how to produce a good crêpe, thin and delicate in texture, well worth eating in its own right with sugar and lemon or simmered in an aromatic syrup, yet substantial enough to wrap around a sweet or savoury filling without coming apart, the variations are child's play.

The pancake pan Choose a frying-pan (5in to 6in in diameter is the usual size) heavy enough to disperse the heat evenly, yet not too heavy, so that you can do the tossing trick with it when so inclined. Rounded sides are an advantage as they make it possible to slip a flexible spatula or knife blade around the edge of the pancake to ease it away from the bottom of the pan.

If you intend to devote a pan exclusively to crêpes, cast-iron or lined copper are both good choices, or heavy aluminium. Before using the pan for the first time it must be 'seasoned': it is washed and dried, heated, coated all over with oil and left to stand overnight. Then, the following day, the excess oil is wiped off and the pan is rubbed clean with salt. Henceforth the pan is never washed again, only wiped clean with kitchen paper between sessions. Anything that sticks to the surface can be rubbed off with a little dry salt.

The pancake batter

A crêpe-type batter is a simple mixture of flour smoothly blended with milk (or milk and water, or cream), with eggs to make the batter rise slightly, a dash of salt, perhaps a pinch of sugar (not too much, though, for sweet batters scorch more easily), a little oil or melted butter to help prevent pancakes sticking – and the merest drop of cognac, rum, wine or beer.

There is practically no difference between a savoury pancake batter and a sweet one.

* The batter must not be overbeaten, as this seems to result in tough pancakes.

* It should be absolutely smooth. If necessary, strain through a fine sieve before use.

* The lighter the batter, the thinner the coating you can spread over the pan and, consequently, the more delicate your pancake will be. Flours vary so much in quality, and eggs in size, that you should always be ready to adjust the liquid specified in the recipe, so that your batter ends up with the consistency of single cream.

* Conversely, if your pancakes tear easily when you handle them, either the batter is too thin, or you have not used enough eggs.

'Resting' the batter

According to time-honoured rules, pancake batters should be left to rest for a couple of hours before they are used. Some people claim that they cannot discern any difference between a batter used straight away and one left to rest. However, one's own experience can be the only guide in such matters, and mine tells me that a batter which is used immediately just will not behave as it should. Resting develops its elasticity so that it runs effortlessly and evenly over the surface of the pan, instead of making ragged streaks that refuse to join up.

Greasing the pan

There are two ways of doing this. In both cases the pan must first be made very hot. Shake a little cold water on to the surface: when the pan is hot enough, it will roll about in little drops and sizzle away almost immediately.

* Then either melt a small knob of butter in the pan, swirling it around quickly to glaze the bottom and sides evenly . . .

* Or simply rub the hot pan all over with a thick wad of kitchen paper dipped in oil or smeared over with lard. (Watch your fingertips!)

The aim is just to grease the pan, *not* to provide fat for the pancake to fry in.

Repeat after every pancake.

Frying the pancake

You now have a very hot, greased pan. Lift away from the heat with your left hand (or your right hand if you're left-handed) and, holding the pan ready to tilt, with your other hand pour a tablespoon of batter into the centre, followed by another tablespoon round the outer perimeter. Immediately start tilting the pan about until the two 'rings' of batter close up to make a thin, even pancake.

* Another method that guarantees paper-thin pancakes, although it is slightly wasteful, pours a good splash of batter into the hot pan from a ladle or jug. As soon as the batter is in the pan, tilt it round and round as before until a thin, even coating has set over the entire surface. Then, if you find you have used too much batter, simply pour the excess back into the bowl as soon as enough has set on the surface, and next time use less.

The 'trail' left behind on the side of the pan can be scraped off with a spatula.

Return the pan to a moderately high heat to cook the pancake until it becomes opaque and dry on top, and little bubbles of air start forming underneath. Then draw a knife blade or flexible spatula round the edges of the pancake to loosen them and either flip it over on the spatula, or give the pan a quick, firm flick to toss it on to the other side. Carry on cooking the pancake for a few seconds longer, but take care not to burn it – the second side always scorches more easily.

* You may find that the first pancake of the batch refuses to form itself properly and sticks badly in spite of careful greasing. Before you start blaming the batter, try making a second pancake. The first one is often a failure, especially when the pan is not kept exclusively for pancakes. In fact, this is a good way of 'seasoning' a pan for the pancakes to come. Just scrape away the offender; rub the pan clean of any burnt scraps with a wad of kitchen paper, and start again.

* It is impossible to colour a pancake evenly on both sides. The second side usually ends up with unattractive dark spots. Make sure when folding or rolling your pancake that this is discreetly turned inwards.

* Finally, the best way to regulate the cooking heat when making pancakes is to draw the *pan* away from the flame or ring when you feel that it's getting too hot and continue cooking the pancake from the heat of the pan itself as it cools down again. This is far more effective than fiddling with the gas or electric controls. I have often found that in a heavy, hot pan I can finish cooking a pancake on one side before I need to return it to the stove for a heat boost.

Stacking pancakes (to be served immediately)

The way you stack your pancakes depends on whether you want them to be tender or slightly crisp. The former are better for rolling or folding as they don't crumble at the edges.

* For soft pancakes, place an upturned soup plate over a pan of hot water and cover it with a clean tea towel folded in four. As soon as the first pancake is ready, slip it out of the pan on to the soup plate and cover it with the cloth. Then repeat with remaining pancakes, stacking them on top of one another.

In this way, the hot steam generated by the pancakes is trapped around them, keeping them warm and softening overcrisp edges.

* For drier pancakes, either stack them as above and keep them hot, uncovered, in a low oven; or cool individually on a wire rack so that all the excess moisture evaporates.

To reheat pancakes

The inverted soup plate over hot water method is equally good for reheating pancakes: cover the plate of pancakes with a bowl and gently reheat the water underneath. In this way the pancakes will warm up gradually without becoming rubbery.

* Stuffed pancakes are usually rolled or folded and then either slipped into a moderate oven or under the grill (not too hot, otherwise the pancakes may burn before the heat has penetrated the filling), or gently fried in butter.

Storing pancakes

Pancakes store well in a refrigerator – which makes them a good standby for the busy host or hostess – and they can also be deep-frozen.

* See that they are quite cold before you put them away, otherwise they may become rubbery when reheated.

* To refrigerate pancakes: wrap the stack of pancakes in an airtight plastic bag or foil. They will keep for several days under mild refrigeration.

* To deep-freeze pancakes: stack the pancakes as above, but this time put a sheet of lightly oiled greaseproof paper between each layer to

prevent them sticking together. Wrap securely in foil or a plastic bag and make sure all the air is expelled before sealing tightly. Deep-frozen pancakes should not be kept longer than about eight weeks.

Savoury pancakes

Basic crêpe batter

Makes 12–15 thin crêpes
4½oz plain flour
Pinch of salt
1 egg
½ pint milk
Olive oil

1 Sift flour and salt into a bowl, and make a well in the centre; break in egg and gradually add milk, stirring from the centre with a wooden spoon to incorporate flour smoothly. When batter is quite free of lumps, stir in 2 teaspoons olive oil. Leave to rest for at least one hour before making *crêpes*.

2 When ready to fry *crêpes*: have ready an upturned soup plate covered with a folded cloth.

3 Heat a small, heavy *crêpe* pan about 6in in diameter. When it is very hot, rub entire surface very lightly with a wad of kitchen paper moistened with oil.

4 Pour about 2 tablespoons batter into centre of hot pan, tilting it quickly so that it coats bottom of pan very thinly and evenly all over before it has had a chance to set. If you find you have used too much batter, pour excess back into the bowl once a thin layer has set on the bottom of the pan, and scrape away the 'trail' it leaves on the side of the pan. Then use a little less batter for the next *crêpe*.

5 Cook steadily for about one minute, drawing a spatula or the point of a knife round edges of *crêpe* to loosen it. As soon as small bubbles begin to form under the *crêpe*, flip it over and cook for sixty to ninety seconds longer.

6 Slip out on to the prepared plate and cover with the cloth.

7 Continue in this manner until you have made twelve *crêpes* in all,
   with an extra one or two as a reserve, stacking them on top of each
   other under the cloth. The pan should be oiled again *very* lightly
   between each *crêpe*.

8 Allow *crêpes* to become quite cold; then store in the refrigerator,
   covered, until needed.

Crêpe batter with beer

Makes 9–10 thin 6in crêpes
3oz plain flour
$\frac{1}{4}$ level teaspoon salt
1 egg
7 fluid oz lager
1 tablespoon melted butter

The taste of lager is not as pronounced as you might suppose in
pancakes made with this batter. It comes through just enough to
complement and give a boost to savoury fillings of ham, shellfish
or cheese.

1 Sift flour and salt into a bowl, and make a well in the centre.

2 Separate egg.

3 Beat egg yolk lightly with lager. Pour into the well slowly, stirring
   from the centre and gradually incorporating flour from sides of
   well with a wooden spoon. Then beat vigorously until smooth.

4 Stir melted butter into batter. Strain through a fine sieve if you
   have not succeeded in eliminating every pocket of flour, and leave
   to rest for at least thirty minutes before frying *crêpes*.

5 Just before using batter, whisk egg white until stiff but not dry and
   fold in carefully but thoroughly with a metal spoon.

6 Cook *crêpes* as directed under *basic crêpe batter*, Steps 3–8, pp.56–7.

Crêpes soufflées au fromage

Serves 6
12 thin *crêpes*, 5in in diameter (p.56)
1oz butter
1oz plain flour
6 fluid oz hot milk
2oz freshly grated Gruyère
Salt and freshly ground black pepper
2 eggs, separated
4 level tablespoons freshly grated Parmesan

This dish is not as awkward as it sounds to prepare as a first course for guests. The *crêpes* can be fried and stacked well in advance, and the filling prepared right up to the point of beating in the egg yolks. Don't go any further, though – the final stages must wait until your guests are just about to sit down to the table.

1 Preheat oven to moderately hot (400°F Mark 6). Butter two large baking sheets.

2 Make the *crêpes*, following the recipe on p.56, and stack them on an upturned soup plate covered with a folded tea towel to keep them moist while you prepare filling.

3 To make filling: melt butter in a thick-bottomed saucepan. Add flour and cook for two to three minutes over a low heat, stirring constantly with a wooden spoon, to make a smooth, pale *roux*. Add milk gradually, beating all the time until sauce is smooth and thick.

4 Beat freshly grated Gruyère into sauce. When sauce is smooth again, season generously with salt and freshly ground black pepper, and allow to cool slightly.

5 When sauce is lukewarm, beat in egg yolks.

6 Whisk egg whites until stiff but not dry, and fold lightly but thoroughly into sauce with a metal spoon or spatula.

7 Put a generous tablespoon of cheese mixture on half of each *crêpe* and fold in two, pressing filling lightly towards the open edge.

8 Transfer *crêpes* to prepared baking sheet with a wide spatula and sprinkle each one with a level teaspoon of grated Parmesan.

9 Bake *crêpes* for twelve to fifteen minutes, or until they are puffed up and crisp golden brown on top. Serve immediately.

Blintzes

Makes 16 blintzes
5oz plain flour, sifted
1 level teaspoon salt
4 eggs, well beaten
½ pint milk or water (see note)
Butter or oil, to fry

A blintz is a thin Jewish pancake, very like a French *crêpe*, although in fact it is Russian in origin. Blintzes are first fried on one side, and then wrapped round a filling and fried again. The filling may be sweet or savoury, and every Jewish housewife will have her own favourite variation. Remember, though, that an Orthodox Jewish cook never serves milk and meat together at the same meal, so that if you are making meat blintzes you must substitute water for milk in the batter, and use oil for frying.

1 Sift flour and salt into a bowl, and make a well in the centre. Combine well beaten eggs with milk or water and pour into the well. Incorporate liquid into flour gradually with a wooden spoon to make a smooth batter.

2 Heat a small knob of butter or oil in a heavy frying-pan 6in in diameter. Pour in enough batter to make a very thin layer, tilting the pan to coat the base evenly. Cook over a steady, low heat on one side only until top of blintz is dry and lightly blistered. Transfer to a clean cloth or a piece of greaseproof paper, fried side up.

3 Repeat until batter is used up, stacking blintzes on top of each other with a sheet of greaseproof paper between each one to prevent them sticking together.

4 To fill blintzes: lay each blintz fried side down and spread a

tablespoon of chosen filling (see below) in centre. Fold vertical sides inwards to enclose filling; then fold up neatly to make an envelope. Blintzes may be prepared in advance and stored in the refrigerator until needed.

5 When ready to serve: fry blintzes in butter or oil over a low, steady heat until they are crisp and golden brown on both sides, and the filling is hot and well cooked.

Meat blintzes

Makes 16 blintzes
1 recipe *blintzes* (p.59)
Oil, for frying

Filling
¾–1lb minced raw beef
1 egg
Salt and freshly ground black pepper
2–3 tablespoons meat stock

1 For authentic Jewish meat blintzes, prepare the batter with water and fry in oil.

2 Mix filling ingredients lightly but thoroughly with a fork.

3 Fill blintzes and fry slowly in oil over a low heat so that meat inside is well cooked. Serve hot.

Bliny

A classic Russian dish: small, thick pancakes made with a mixture of buckwheat and plain flour, raised with yeast. Serve them straight from the pan. Each guest helps himself to a pancake and assembles it as follows: first a brushing of melted butter, then some smoked fish, e.g. salmon, trout or even skinned and boned buckling (or substitute a generous layer of salted herring butter, p.62 and finally a dollop of soured cream.

On extra-special occasions, serve bliny with black caviar.

Bliny

Makes 12–14

8oz plain flour
8oz buckwheat flour
2 level teaspoons dried yeast
1 pint lukewarm milk
Generous pinch of sugar
2 eggs, separated
1oz butter, melted
Salt
3oz fat, for frying

1 Sift plain flour into a large bowl and buckwheat flour into a smaller one.

2 Dissolve yeast according to instructions on the can or packet, using a little of the lukewarm milk sweetened with a pinch of sugar.

3 Make a hollow in the centre of the plain flour; pour in dissolved yeast and work into flour gradually, beating with a wooden spoon, and adding enough of the remaining milk to make a thick, smooth batter. Cover bowl and leave batter to rise in a warm place until light and bubbly, and doubled in bulk.

4 Beat in buckwheat flour and enough of the remaining milk to make a batter with the consistency of double cream. When batter is absolutely smooth again, beat in egg yolks, melted butter and salt, to taste.

5 Whisk egg whites until stiff but not dry. Fold them lightly but thoroughly into batter with a spatula or a metal spoon, and leave to rise until almost doubled in bulk again.

6 Heat a heavy frying-pan 4in or 5in in diameter and brush lightly with a little fat. Ladle $\frac{1}{4}$in batter into pan, swirling to distribute it evenly, and cook over a steady, moderate heat until underside is golden and little bubbles have formed all over the top; then flip over with a spatula and brown the other side.

7 Continue in this manner until batter is used up, greasing pan every
   time and either serving bliny straight from the frying-pan, or
   stacking them on a large dish over a pan of simmering water,
   covered with a clean napkin, until they are all prepared. Serve very
   hot.

Salted herring butter

Makes about $\frac{1}{2}$lb
$\frac{1}{2}$lb salted herrings
2 hard-boiled egg yolks
4oz unsalted butter, softened

To serve with hot bliny (see p.61), as a canapé spread, or with
baked potatoes or potato pancakes (see below).

Herrings pickled in vinegar or other acid are of no use for this
recipe. You must get real salted herrings from a barrel and you will
probably find them at a delicatessen specialising in Eastern
European food.

1 Desalt herrings thoroughly by soaking them in a bowl of cold water
   for at least twenty-four hours, changing water frequently. It is
   advisable to leave them under running water for the first half-hour.

2 Drain herrings thoroughly and pat dry with kitchen paper. Then
   fillet them, removing every scrap of skin and bone.

3 Chop herrings finely and pound smoothly to a paste in a mortar,
   together with hard-boiled egg yolks.

4 Turn paste into a bowl. Add softened butter and beat until very
   smooth and fluffy. Shape into a neat brick and chill until firm.

Polish potato pancakes

Serves 3–4 (12 pancakes)
1lb floury potatoes
1 egg

1 level tablespoon plain flour
Salt
Lard or butter and oil, for frying

These hearty pancakes are not only economical, but very versatile, too: you can serve them savoury, on their own, spread with a herring sauce or as an accompaniment to casseroled beef; or sweet – traditionally sprinkled with sugar and topped with a dollop of soured cream.

1 Line a sieve with a double thickness of muslin and set it over a bowl.

2 Peel, wash and dry potatoes, and grate them very finely into the muslin-lined sieve.

3 Draw up sides of muslin and gently press excess moisture out into the bowl.

4 Allow liquid in the bowl to stand for a few minutes; then pour it off carefully, leaving behind the starch, which will have settled on the bottom.

5 Combine grated potatoes with potato starch. Add the egg, flour, and salt to taste, and blend thoroughly with a wooden spoon. Potato mixture should be quite thick.

6 Fry pancakes two or three at a time. In a large frying-pan, melt 2 or 3 tablespoons lard (or a combination of butter and oil). When sizzling, drop in a tablespoon of potato mixture for each pancake and, with a spatula or the back of a spoon, spread out into a thin oval (the thinner the layer, the crisper will be the pancake). Fry on one side until pancake is crisp and golden underneath; then flip over and continue to fry until other side is golden.

7 Drain pancakes thoroughly on absorbent paper. They are at their best served straight from the pan, but you can keep them hot in a slow oven until you have finished frying them. Do not lay them on top of each other, though, or they will turn limp and rubbery.

Chappatis

Serves 4
Wholewheat flour
½ level teaspoon salt
Butter (optional)

1 Sift 8oz wholewheat flour and salt into a bowl.

2 Gradually sprinkle on about ⅓ pint cold water, working flour with your fingertips to make a stiff dough which you can just knead. Knead until smooth; roll into a ball and leave to rest for thirty minutes, covered with a damp cloth.

3 Dust your hands lightly with extra wholewheat flour and knead dough vigorously for two to three minutes until it loses its stickiness.

4 Divide dough into eight equal pieces. Flour your rolling pin and surface generously, and roll each piece into a thin circle 5in in diameter.

5 Heat an ungreased griddle or heavy frying-pan until very hot and cook chappatis for two to three minutes on each side until brown spots appear on the floury surface.

6 Serve chappatis very hot just as they are or lightly spread with butter on one side only.

Parathas

Serves 4
Wholewheat flour
½ level teaspoon salt
5oz softened butter
Freshly ground black pepper
Ground cumin

A traditional accompaniment for curry.

1 Sift 10oz wholewheat flour and salt into a bowl.

2 Rub in 1oz softened butter until thoroughly incorporated. Then gradually sprinkle on about $\frac{1}{4}$ pint cold water, working and kneading mixture to a smooth, stiff dough. Roll into a ball. Cover bowl with a damp cloth and put dough aside to rest for thirty minutes.

3 Divide dough into four equal pieces. Reserve 1oz of the remaining butter for frying the *parathas*, and put the rest on a plate.

4 Dust your rolling pin and surface with a little extra wholewheat flour, and roll each piece of dough into a thin circle about 7in in diameter. Spread with a little butter; fold circle in half and seal edges by pinching them firmly between your fingers. Then spread with more butter, fold in half again to make a triangle, and seal edges once more. Finally, roll each triangle into a circle, this time making it about 6in in diameter.

5 To fry *parathas*: heat a heavy frying-pan thoroughly and grease with some of the reserved butter. Fry each *paratha* for two to three minutes on each side until golden and rather flaky.

6 Dust hot *parathas* with freshly ground black pepper and a pinch of ground cumin, and serve immediately.

Bacon pancakes

Serves 4
4oz plain flour
Salt
1 egg, lightly beaten
$\frac{1}{4}$ pint milk
1 tablespoon oil
4 level teaspoons butter
12–16 slices streaky bacon

1 Sift flour into a bowl with a pinch of salt and make a well in the centre.

2 Pour in lightly beaten egg and the milk, and stir with a wooden spoon, working from the centre of the well and incorporating flour very gradually from sides until blended to a perfectly smooth

batter. Stir in oil. The batter should have the consistency of thick cream. If too thick, beat in a little more milk. (Note: If batter is lumpy in spite of all precautions, strain it through a fine sieve.) Put aside to rest for at least one hour.

3 Preheat oven to fairly hot (425°F Mark 7).

4 The pancakes can be baked in four individual round heatproof dishes 6in in diameter, or in a 9in by 11in roasting tin. Melt butter in the chosen dish(es) and fry bacon slices slowly until crisp, allowing three or four per person according to size.

5 Pour over batter.

6 Bake pancakes for twenty to twenty-five minutes until puffy and golden brown. Serve very hot.

Crisp-fried pancake rolls with chicken or beef

Serves 4–6
12 *crêpes*, 6in in diameter (p.56)
1 egg
Salt and freshly ground black pepper
2–3oz fine stale breadcrumbs
Butter and olive oil, for frying

Chicken filling
1 Spanish onion, very finely chopped
1 tablespoon olive oil
8oz cooked chicken meat, coarsely minced
4 level tablespoons finely chopped parsley
$\frac{1}{2}$ level teaspoon dried mixed herbs
2 egg yolks, lightly beaten
4 level tablespoons double cream
4 tablespoons milk or chicken stock
4 drops Tabasco
Salt and freshly ground black pepper

Beef filling
1 Spanish onion, very finely chopped
1 tablespoon olive oil

12oz cooked beef, coarsely minced
6 level tablespoons finely chopped parsley
$\frac{3}{4}$ level teaspoon dried mixed herbs
2 egg yolks, lightly beaten
3 tablespoons milk or beef stock
$\frac{1}{2}$–1 teaspoon Worcestershire or soy sauce
$1\frac{1}{2}$ level tablespoons concentrated tomato purée
Salt and freshly ground black pepper

Serve these crisp-fried pancake rolls with bowls of steaming hot,
clear consommé, or as a supper dish, accompanied by a tomato or
mushroom sauce.

They are a very useful way of using up left-over cooked meats.

1 Prepare *crêpes* in advance. They should be quite thin, but sound
 and free of holes.

2 The method for both fillings is exactly the same: sauté finely
 chopped onion in olive oil for three or four minutes until transparent
 and lightly coloured. Turn into a mixing bowl.

3 Combine with remaining ingredients and blend thoroughly,
 adding salt and freshly ground black pepper, to taste.

4 Lay a *crêpe* flat. Put 2 level tablespoons meat filling in the centre,
 moulding it into a small, thick sausage with your fingers (filling
 will be stiff enough to hold its shape). Fold two sides of *crêpe* in over
 filling and roll up into a neat, secure parcel. Repeat with remaining
 crêpes and filling.

5 Beat egg lightly with a tablespoon of water in a shallow dish. Add
 a pinch each of salt and freshly ground black pepper.

6 Coat each *crêpe* roll completely with beaten egg, allowing excess
 to drain off, and cover with fine breadcrumbs. (At this stage the
 rolls can be put aside under mild refrigeration until just before
 serving.)

7 When ready to serve: heat equal quantities of butter and oil in a
 large, heavy frying-pan and fry *crêpe* rolls gently for seven or eight

minutes until crisp and golden brown on all sides. (Make sure filling has heated right through.) Drain well and serve immediately.

Sweet pancakes

Basic batter for dessert crêpes

Makes twelve 6in crêpes
4oz plain flour
Pinch of salt
1 level teaspoon castor sugar
1 egg
8 fluid oz milk
1 tablespoon corn or peanut oil
1 tablespoon brandy

1 Sift flour, salt and castor sugar into a bowl, and make a well in the centre.

2 Beat egg lightly and pour into the well. Slowly add milk, stirring from the centre with a wooden spoon and gradually incorporating flour from sides of well. Then beat batter until smooth.

3 Stir in oil and brandy. Strain batter through a fine sieve if necessary and leave to rest for at least 1 hour before making *crêpes*.

4 Cook *crêpes* as directed under *basic crêpe batter*, Steps 3–8, pp.56–7.

Kirsch butter crêpes

Serve 2 per person. The filling is very rich
8 *crêpes*, 6in in diameter (see recipe above)
2 level tablespoons icing sugar

Kirsch butter
4 level tablespoons unsalted butter
4 level tablespoons castor sugar
3 tablespoons Kirsch

1 Prepare Kirsch butter: soften butter in a bowl. Add castor sugar and beat until very light and fluffy. When mixture is almost white, add

Kirsch a little at a time, beating vigorously with a wire whisk.
Scrape butter into a mound and chill until firm.

2 To assemble *crêpes*: put an eighth of the butter at one end of each
crêpe. Roll up and fold ends under to close the parcel.

3 Pack *crêpes* tightly side by side in a fireproof dish with folded ends
underneath. *Crêpes* may be left like this in a cool place for several
hours.

4 Just before serving, sift icing sugar over the top of the *crêpes* and
place under a hot, preheated grill until glazed and golden. Serve
immediately.

Crêpes suzette

Serves 4
12 *crêpes*, 5in to 6in in diameter (p.68)

Orange butter
4oz unsalted butter, softened
2oz castor sugar
Finely grated rind of 1 large orange
2 tablespoons orange liqueur
5 tablespoons orange juice

To flame
1 level tablespoon castor sugar
2 tablespoons orange liqueur
2 tablespoons brandy

1 Prepare *crêpes* in advance. They should be thin, but not paper-thin.

2 Prepare orange butter: in a bowl, cream softened butter with sugar
and grated orange rind, and when fluffy, beat in orange liqueur
and juice a little at a time. The butter will probably curdle, but this
does not matter.

3 Melt the orange butter in a chafing dish, a large electric frying-pan,
or a heavy frying-pan (the pancakes might scorch in a thin one).

Let it bubble over a low heat for three or four minutes until slightly reduced.

4 Keeping the heat low, immerse a *crêpe* in the bubbling butter and, with the aid of a fork and spoon, fold it in half and then in half again, and push it to the side of the pan. Repeat with remaining *crêpes*.

5 To flame: when all the *crêpes* are in the pan, sprinkle surface with castor sugar and pour over orange liqueur mixed with brandy.

Light a match and, standing well clear, set the alcohol alight. Remove pan from heat. Keep spooning the flaming syrup over the *crêpes* until the alcohol burns itself out. Serve immediately.

Crêpes soufflées au citron

Serves 6
12 *crêpes*, 6in in diameter (p.68)
Sifted icing sugar
1 tablespoon each cognac and Grand Marnier (optional)

Soufflé mixture
1oz plain flour
2oz granulated sugar
4 egg yolks
$\frac{1}{4}$ pint milk
2 lemons
3 egg whites

Souffléed *crêpes* make a spectacular dish for a dinner party. The pancakes can be cooked and stacked, and Steps 1 and 2 of the soufflé mixture completed in the morning. Steps 3, 4, 5 and 6 should be seen to before you sit down to the table, leaving Steps 7 to 11 until just before serving.

1 Prepare soufflé mixture: combine flour with sugar, 2 egg yolks and 4 tablespoons of the milk in a bowl. Bring remaining milk to the boil and pour over flour mixture, beating vigorously. Return to the pan and cook over a low heat, stirring constantly, for two or three minutes longer. Remove from heat.

2 Grate the rind of the 2 lemons very finely and beat into the mixture, together with 1 tablespoon lemon juice.

3 Clear a surface and lay out pancakes side by side. If necessary, trim ragged edges with a pair of scissors. Select a shallow baking dish large enough to hold all the pancakes folded in half, and suitable for serving at table.

4 Put egg whites in the bowl of your electric mixer (or have them ready in a bowl with a hand beater beside it). Have icing sugar and a small sieve ready to use. Assemble cognac and Grand Marnier, a metal ladle and a box of matches if you intend to flame the *crêpes*.

5 Beat remaining 2 egg yolks into soufflé mixture.

6 Preheat oven to fairly hot (425°F Mark 7).

7 Just before serving: whisk egg whites until stiff but not dry, and fold them into soufflé mixture with a large metal spoon or spatula.

8 Lay a trimmed pancake in the baking dish; put 3 level tablespoons soufflé mixture in centre and fold pancake in two so that top half overlaps bottom half by about ½in.

9 Fill all twelve pancakes in this manner. Dust all over with icing sugar and bake for ten minutes, or until puffed and golden.

10 Meanwhile, if you intend to flame the *crêpes*, heat the ladle in hot water. Dry it thoroughly. Pour in cognac and Grand Marnier, and swirl around for a few seconds to warm them gently.

11 As soon as *crêpes* come out of the oven, set a match to the alcohol and, when flames are burning brightly, dribble them up one row of *crêpes* and down the other. Serve at once.

Coffee–chocolate crêpes

Serves 6
4oz plain flour
Castor sugar

Pinch of salt
1 level tablespoon powdered chocolate
1 level tablespoon instant coffee powder
2 eggs
¾ pint milk
2 tablespoons melted butter
Oil
½ pint double cream, chilled
1 tablespoon rum

1 Sift flour into a bowl with 1 level tablespoon castor sugar, the salt, powdered chocolate and instant coffee. Make a well in the centre.

2 Beat eggs lightly. Pour into well and start stirring from the centre with a wooden spoon, adding milk in a thin stream as you gradually incorporate flour from sides of well with your spoon.

3 When batter is smoothly blended, beat in melted butter and strain through a fine sieve to ensure there are no pockets of unblended flour left. The batter should have the consistency of thin cream. Allow it to stand for at least two hours before frying *crêpes*.

4 Heat a 6in *crêpe* pan until a drop of water shaken on to it sizzles and rolls about on contact. Rub base and sides of hot pan with a wad of kitchen paper dipped in oil.

5 Pour about 2 tablespoons batter into the pan, and quickly swirl it around so that base is entirely covered before batter has had a chance to set.

6 Cook over a fairly high heat for a minute or two until *crêpe* is coloured and slightly crisp underneath; then flip it over with a palette knife and cook for a further one or two minutes.

7 Continue to make pancakes in this manner until batter is all used up, stacking them on top of each other on an upturned soup plate over a pan of hot water, and oiling the pan lightly for every pancake.

8 Just before serving, whip chilled cream until very thick and flavour with rum and a little castor sugar, to taste.

9 Spread each *crêpe* with rum-flavoured cream and roll up. Serve immediately before cream starts melting from warmth of *crêpes*.

Note: Poached pear slices make a delicious garnish for these *crêpes*. For the above portion of *crêpes*, allow 3 ripe pears, peeled, cored and thinly sliced, and poached in a vanilla-flavoured syrup until tender but not mushy.

Souffléed apple pancakes

Serves 4–6 (2 pancakes per person)

Pancake batter
2½oz plain flour
2 level tablespoons castor sugar
Salt
3 eggs
½ pint milk
¼ teaspoon finely grated lemon rind
Few drops of vanilla essence

3 crisp dessert apples
Lemon juice
Oil or butter
Sifted icing sugar
Ground cinnamon

1 To make pancake batter: sift flour, castor sugar and ¼ level teaspoon salt into a large bowl, and make a well in the centre.

2 Break 1 egg into a bowl. Separate 2 remaining eggs, adding yolks to the bowl with the whole egg, and putting whites aside for the moment.

3 Beat whole egg lightly with yolks. Pour into the flour mixture.

4 Gradually pour in milk, stirring from the centre with a wooden spoon and incorporating flour from sides of well a little at a time to prevent lumps forming. When batter is smooth and well blended, add finely grated lemon rind and a few drops of vanilla, to taste, and continue to beat vigorously for a minute or two longer. Leave batter to rest while you prepare apples.

5 Peel, core and slice apples thinly into a bowl with a little water acidulated with lemon juice to prevent them discolouring.

6 When ready to make pancakes, add a small pinch of salt to the egg whites and whisk them until stiff but not dry. Fold gently into batter with a metal spoon or spatula.

7 Heat a 6in *crêpe* pan over a moderate heat and either brush bottom and sides with a wad of kitchen paper dipped in oil, or melt a small knob of butter in it, swirling it around so that the entire surface is coated.

8 Pour 2 to 3 tablespoons batter into the pan, tilting it quickly back and forth to coat entire surface before batter has had a chance to set. Cook steadily over a moderate heat for about one minute until pancake is set and golden underneath.

9 Cover each pancake with some drained apple slices and pour another 2 or 3 tablespoons batter over it. Then, with a wide spatula, turn pancake over and continue to fry until other side is golden brown. Pancake should remain slightly creamy in the centre.

10 Fold pancake over in two or three and transfer to a heated serving dish. Dust with icing sugar and sprinkle with a good pinch of cinnamon. Keep hot.

11 Continue in this manner until batter and apples are used up, greasing pan with oil or butter before every pancake. Serve immediately.

Polish cottage cheese pancakes

Serves 4–6
12 thin *crêpes*, 6in in diameter (p.68)
Butter

Filling
2 level tablespoons sultanas or raisins
8oz cottage cheese
2oz unsalted butter, softened

2 egg yolks
2 level tablespoons castor sugar
¼ teaspoon vanilla essence
Finely grated rind of 1 small lemon
2 teaspoons lemon juice
¼ level teaspoon ground cinnamon

Topping
2 level tablespoons icing sugar
2 level tablespoons unsalted butter

1 To make filling: cover sultanas or raisins with boiling water and put them aside to plump up and soften for a few minutes.

2 Drain off any excess liquid from cottage cheese. Rub cheese through a fine sieve into a bowl.

3 Add softened butter and beat vigorously with a wooden spoon until smoothly blended.

4 Beat in remaining ingredients, together with the soaked sultanas, drained and pressed dry against the sides of a sieve.

5 Divide cheese mixture between prepared *crêpes*. Roll them up and tuck ends under to seal in filling.

6 Butter a heatproof rectangular dish and arrange *crêpe* rolls in it side by side. They may be left like this for several hours, covered with foil, in the refrigerator.

7 When ready to serve: dust *crêpes* with sifted icing sugar and dot with flakes of butter.

8 Slip dish under a hot, preheated grill for five to seven minutes, or until *crêpes* are golden and bubbling on top, and hot through. Serve immediately.

Note: Instead of grilling the *crêpes*, you can fry them gently in butter until crisp and golden on the outside, and thoroughly hot in the centre.

Kaiserschmarrn

Serves 4–6
2–3oz raisins or sultanas
12 pancakes (not too thin) (p.68)
2–3oz blanched almonds, slivered
3 level tablespoons butter
1–2 level tablespoons icing sugar

1 Cover raisins or sultanas with boiling water and leave to plump up and soften for fifteen minutes.

2 Meanwhile, cut the pancakes into ½in squares or diamonds.

3 Drain soaked raisins or sultanas thoroughly and toss with pancake pieces and almond slivers in a bowl.

4 Melt butter in a frying-pan. When it is foaming, add pancake mixture and sauté over a moderate heat for three to four minutes, tossing with a fork, until hot and golden brown.

5 Pile mixture into a heatproof serving dish. Sift icing sugar over the top.

6 Slip dish under a very hot, preheated grill for about thirty seconds so that sugar caramelises without burning. Serve immediately.

Apple blintzes

Serves 3–4
½ recipe (8) *blintzes* (p.59)
2–3 tart eating apples
1½ level tablespoons ground almonds
1 egg white
1 level tablespoon icing sugar
¼ level teaspoon ground cinnamon
Lemon juice (optional)
Cinnamon sugar, to serve

1 Prepare and fry blintzes, following directions on p.59.

2 Peel, core and chop apples finely.

3 Add ground almonds, the egg white, icing sugar and cinnamon, and toss until well mixed. Add a little lemon juice if apples are too sweet, more icing sugar if they seem tart.

4 Fill blintzes and fry as described in the master recipe.

5 Serve hot with cinnamon sugar.

Cherry blintzes

Serves 3–4
½ recipe (8) *blintzes* (p.59)
8oz fresh or canned pitted cherries
1 level tablespoon plain flour
¼ level teaspoon ground cinnamon
¼ level teaspoon castor sugar
Finely grated rind of ½ lemon
Soured cream or cinnamon sugar, to serve

1 Prepare and fry blintzes, following direction on p.59.

2 Toss cherries with flour, cinnamon, sugar and grated lemon rind until well mixed.

3 Fill blintzes and fry as described in the master recipe.

4 Serve hot with thick soured cream or cinnamon sugar.

Fish and shellfish

Fish can be one of the most delicious dishes on your menu. Treat it gently; flavour it with fresh fish stock, lemon juice, dry white wine or a delicate sauce; and above all don't overcook it. You'll find that you will soon enjoy cooking fish dishes. After all, fish is inexpensive; it is never tough; and it's wonderfully easy to cook, once you know how.

Many cooks think that there is nothing in the world as difficult to cook really well as fish, for its delicate flavour is so easily lost, and its light creamy flakiness so quickly destroyed. Indeed, until fairly recently in this country we did *not* know how to prepare fish properly. It was usually overcooked – boiled to a tasteless rag in water with a little vinegar added – or fried in breadcrumbs, oatmeal or just plain flour until it was crisp and hard, which entirely ruined its delicate texture and flavour.

How to choose fish in the market

The first step towards cooking fish superbly is knowing how to recognise healthy, fresh fish in the market. It is surprisingly easy. Just look for the following indications.

You can tell that a fish is fresh when its eye is rounded and bright, not sunken and dull; when the body is firm, almost stiff, not weak and flabby; when the scales are close fitting, and when the body leaves no imprint when you press it with your fingers.

One of the best indications of a really fresh fish is its mild odour. Learn to distinguish the mild odour of a healthy fish from the strong smell of stale fish.

Do not buy fish

If it has too strong an odour; if the scales come off easily; if the eye is sunken in its socket; if the fish droops weakly over the counter; and if the area over the stomach or around the vent is green or blackish in colour.

Keeping fish

Fresh fish should be used as soon as possible

If you are going to serve it on the following day, wash it, pat it dry, wrap it loosely in waxed paper and keep it in the refrigerator until ready to use.

Keep frozen fish, unopened, at a ten-degree temperature. I prefer to thaw frozen fish in the refrigerator. Cook as soon as it is thawed. If it is frozen fillets or fingers, I sometimes cook them while still frozen. In either case, do not refreeze frozen fish after it has thawed. It will lose both flavour and texture.

Keep fish away from butter, sweets and puddings to prevent the fish affecting delicately flavoured foods.

To steam fish

Oval steamer method There are oval steamers on the market for poultry, meats or vegetables that double wonderfully well as fish steamers. Consisting of oval double saucepans with perforated bottoms to allow the steam to rise, and covers to keep steam in, they make a remarkable fish steamer.

To steam a fish in an oval steamer: place fish in a well-buttered oval baking dish that just fits inside the steamer, allowing about an inch round for the steam to rise. Sprinkle with 2 tablespoons each finely chopped onion and mushrooms; moisten with 6 tablespoons dry white wine, canned clam juice or well-flavoured fish stock, and place over boiling water to which you have added a clove or two of garlic for flavour. Cover tightly and steam until fish flakes easily with a fork.

Fish kettle method For a larger fish – or a greater number of small fish, fish steaks or fillets – use a long fish kettle complete with cover and perforated rack. To transform this kettle into a steamer, place rack on heat-proof porcelain ramekins to allow liquid to boil below rack and the steam to rise.

Most fish kettles are big enough to poach or steam a young salmon, or a large centre cut of a larger salmon, a number of lobsters, plenty of oysters or clams, 6–12 trout, several chickens, or a large platter of meat and vegetables in the Chinese manner. Try flavouring your steaming liquid with sliced onion, several bay leaves, 10–12 coriander seeds, 10–12 peppercorns, a generous amount of salt, several garlic cloves and a little dry white wine. Season the fish with salt and freshly ground black pepper, and stuff cavity with stalks of fresh or dried fennel, bay leaves, thyme, lemon slices and garlic. You'll find steamed fish is delicious.

To poach fish

One of the easiest ways of cooking fish fillets and small fish steaks or cutlets was taught to me in Paris by the great French restaurateur, René Lasserre. His easy method is to the art of poaching what 'oven-frying' is to deep-frying. So I call it 'oven-poaching'.

To 'oven-poach' fillets of sole for four: butter a shallow heatproof gratin dish generously; sprinkle it with a level tablespoon or two of chopped mushrooms (stems will do) and the same amount of chopped shallots; lay in your fish fillets which you have first anointed with a little lemon juice and seasoned with salt and freshly ground black pepper to taste. Sprinkle the fillets with a little more chopped mushrooms and shallots and cover them with the bones and trimmings of the fish to give added flavour and moisture. Place a piece of well-buttered aluminium foil over fish and cook in a hot oven (450°F Mark 8) until the fish is tender and opaque (about eight to twelve minutes).

Another variation on this same recipe just adds 2–4 tablespoons each reduced fish stock and dry white wine.

To serve: lift fish out carefully, draining it well, and place it on a heated serving dish. Keep warm. Thicken pan liquids slightly with a *beurre manié* or with an egg yolk mixed with a little double cream and lemon juice, to taste. Serve with the fish. This manner of cooking fish is guaranteed to bring out the utmost in flavour of the most delicate fish.

Fish stock from trimmings

A well-flavoured fish stock can be made at little expense or effort from fish trimmings. This stock can be used for cooking the fish or for making a sauce to accompany it. There is no comparison between a sauce made with a well-flavoured fish stock and one in which milk or water forms the liquid part. So if you have your fish filleted by your fishmonger, ask for the fish trimmings to be included with the fish.

To make the stock, wash the trimmings, discarding any black-looking skin, and break the bones in pieces. Put them in an enamelled saucepan with just enough water to cover them, and add a few parsley stalks, a sliced onion, a few white peppercorns and a little salt. Simmer for at least half an hour and then strain ready for use. White wine may be added with the water.

Any white fish or the trimmings of white fish – haddock, cod, halibut or flounder – may be used for fish stock. Mackerel, herring and salmon are too oily and too strong in flavour. Uncooked trimmings, however, make a better stock than those which have already been cooked. A cod's head is an economical foundation for a well-flavoured fish stock. And always ask your fishmonger for heads and bones of sole. I also like to add a lobster shell, or the heads and shells of prawns and shrimps, when available.

To grill fish

Wash and clean fish; dry lightly and score the skin across diagonally on both sides to prevent it cracking during cooking. Season with salt and freshly ground black pepper, and brush with olive oil or melted butter. Or marinate fish for two hours before cooking in equal quantities of olive oil and dry white wine with a little finely chopped garlic and a crumbled bay leaf or two. Or the fish may be split open, the bones removed, and then lightly coated with flour, egg and breadcrumbs, or fine oatmeal.

Always heat the grid thoroughly and grease it well before you place the fish on it. Keep the fish rather close to the fire while cooking or it will become flabby. Cook fish for eight to twelve minutes according to its thickness, and turn it at least once during cooking time. I like to serve grilled fish with lemon quarters and *maître d'hôtel* or *fines herbes* butter.

Charcoal–grilled fish

The odorous smoke from a charcoal or wood fire – with the scent of burning dried fennel stalks, sprigs of thyme or rosemary, or a sprig of bay leaves – makes grilled fish a dish 'fit for a king'. Use a hinged grill when grilling fish over an open fire so that you can turn your fish easily without danger of breaking its tender flesh.

Flour and oil all fish lightly before grilling, and if you are using fish steaks or fish fillets, be sure to baste them frequently with olive oil and lemon juice during cooking time.

Whole fish, with skins intact, require less attention. Stuff cavities of fish with herbs before grilling them – a selection of fennel, parsley and thyme – and then baste them with olive oil and lemon juice as they grill.

To bake fish

The simplest method of baking fish is to place it in a well-buttered heatproof baking dish with a little finely chopped onion and mushroom, and salt and freshly ground black pepper, to taste; cover it with buttered waxed paper or foil, and cook in a moderate oven (375°F Mark 5) until fish flakes with a fork. The fish may be served with or without sauce.

Otherwise the fish may be first poached for a few minutes in a little fish stock and then baked *au gratin* with butter, finely chopped parsley, mushrooms and shallots, and sprinkled with freshly grated breadcrumbs and Parmesan cheese; or a little Béchamel or Velouté

sauce may be poured around the fish before it is dotted with butter
and sprinkled with chopped parsley, mushrooms, shallots and cheese.

To fry fish

When properly fried, fish should be a light golden brown and dry
and crisp in texture, as free from fat as if it had never touched it.
I like to deep-fry fish in a combination of lard and oil to give
added flavour; for pan-frying or oven-frying I use butter or olive
oil, or combination of the two.

Small fish are better fried whole, large ones should be filleted or
cut into steaks or cutlets.

I like to 'flavour' fish fillets or steaks with a little lemon juice and
dry white wine seasoned generously with salt and pepper about an
hour before frying.

To fry well, fish should be as dry as possible. So, pat fish dry with
a clean cloth or paper towel before coating it with seasoned flour,
fine oatmeal or cornmeal, beaten egg and dry breadcrumbs, or a
frying batter. This coating serves two purposes: (1) to keep fat
from entering the fish while it is immersed in the hot cooking fat
or oil; and (2) to add a flavoursome crunchy coating to the fried
fish, which adds enormously to the delicately flavoured flesh within.

If seasoned flour, or flour and milk, are used as a coating, apply it
just before the fish is to be cooked, or the flour will become moist
and the fish will not fry well. Batter, too, should be applied only
at the last moment. But the fish may be coated with egg and dry
breadcrumbs some time before it is to be fried – even the night
before if the fish is to be served for breakfast.

Pan-frying fish

This method of cooking sautés delicately flavoured fish such as
sole, plaice, brill or trout in $\frac{1}{8}$in butter in a frying-pan. Finely
chopped parsley, lemon juice or slivered almonds are sometimes
added to the sauce obtained. It is a good idea to add a little olive
oil to the butter first to keep it from browning during the cooking

process. Allow it to sizzle; lay in the prepared fish and cook gently, making sure that the entire bottom surface of the fish is in contact with the butter. When the fish begins to take on colour, add more butter. Then turn the fish with a fish slice or a palette knife and continue to cook until it flakes easily with a fork.

Oven-frying fish

Heat the oven to 400°F (Mark 6). Cover the bottom of a shallow baking dish with butter and a little olive oil (about $\frac{1}{4}$in), and heat the dish in the oven until the butter sizzles. Brush fish with olive oil or melted butter and roll it in dry breadcrumbs mixed with chopped fresh herbs (parsley, chervil, chives, etc.) and a little grated lemon rind. Cook in the oven until tender, turning once during cooking time.

Deep-frying fish

Deep-fried fish should never be greasy. Thus the temperature of the fat or oil used for frying is of prime importance. It must be hot enough to seal the protective coating of flour, oatmeal, cornmeal, egg and breadcrumbs, batter or pastry at the very moment of immersion. This prevents grease from penetrating the food and keeps in the flavour and juices of the fish. Deep-frying is simple when you know how. Vegetable fats and oils are the most pleasant to use – with a little lard added for extra flavour. Test the heat of your fat with an inch cube of day-old bread. If the temperature is right for deep-frying, the bread will brown on both sides in about forty seconds.

Do not put too many pieces of fish into the fat or oil at one time, or it will cool down so much that it will soak through the coating or batter. If you use a frying basket, do not let pieces overlap or the fish will not cook through. Cook until fish are golden brown; then lift out and drain on paper towels.

If a frying basket is not used, a perforated spoon or skimmer is best for lifting out fish.

1 Use enough fat or oil to cover fish completely.

2 Do not allow fat to smoke or boil.

3 The temperature of the fat should vary as little as possible during cooking.

4 If fat becomes too hot or begins to smoke, drop a slice of raw potato into it to reduce temperature.

5 Always allow the fat or oil to reheat before adding a fresh lot of fish.

6 If you plunge fish into the fat a second time, the temperature of the second cooking should be higher than that of the first.

Oven-baked fish

Oven-baked fish – whether you use the basic method below, or add a little dry white wine, fish or chicken stock and one or more exotic aromatics – brings out the best in a whole fish, or a thick steak of cod, halibut, turbot or flounder. Try, too, fillets of your favourite fish, wrapped around a savoury stuffing, and baked in the same manner.

You'll find that *oven-baked fish* becomes one of your most useful party dishes.

First of all, try the *simple baked fish* recipe below, using 1½in thick steaks of turbot, halibut or cod.

The simplest method of baking fish you've ever tried

1 Butter a baking dish generously with softened butter. Then sprinkle the dish with 2 tablespoons each of chopped celery, chopped mushroom stalks, chopped onion and chopped carrot. Season vegetables with salt and freshly ground black pepper.

2 Lay the fish steaks on the vegetables and season with salt and freshly ground black pepper and lemon juice, to taste.

3 Lay fish bones and trimmings over fish, if available, to give added flavour to the pan juices. (Make a habit of asking your fishmonger for some bones and trimmings of sole when you purchase any fish, for this very reason).

4 Cover tightly with a well-buttered piece of aluminium foil and bake fish in a preheated moderately hot oven (400°F Mark 6) for twenty minutes.

5 Remove foil and fish bones and trimmings; baste fish well with the liquids formed and bake for another ten minutes, or until lightly browned.

6 Serve fish steaks with boiled new potatoes and strained pan juices to which you have added $\frac{1}{4}$lb butter and 2 tablespoons finely chopped parsley, and lemon juice to taste.

Fisherman's pie

Serves 6
1$\frac{1}{2}$–2lb smoked haddock fillets
Milk
Butter
2 level tablespoons flour
$\frac{1}{2}$ pint double cream
Freshly ground black pepper
Freshly grated nutmeg
4oz peeled shrimps or prawns
4 scallops, cleaned and sliced
Juice of $\frac{1}{2}$ lemon
24 mussels, steamed open (see p.128)
6–8oz shortcrust pastry
1 egg yolk beaten with 1 tablespoon milk, to glaze

1 Soak smoked haddock fillets in cold water for two hours. Drain them and place them in a saucepan with equal quantities of milk and water to cover. Bring to a fast boil. Remove pan from heat; cover and leave for fifteen minutes. Then carefully drain haddock, reserving cooking liquor.

2 Melt 2oz butter in the top of a double saucepan; stir in flour and cook over boiling water for three minutes, stirring constantly, to make a smooth, pale *roux*.

3 Gradually add cream and ½ pint of the hot haddock liquor, stirring vigorously to prevent lumps forming, and continue to cook over boiling water, stirring occasionally, for about thirty minutes, or until sauce is thick and smooth. Season to taste with freshly ground black pepper and a pinch of freshly grated nutmeg.

4 In a frying pan, sauté peeled shrimps or prawns and sliced scallops in a little butter for just two to three minutes until golden. Sprinkle with lemon juice. Remove from heat.

5 Butter a deep, 4 pint pie dish.

6 Remove skin and any remaining bones from haddock fillets, and separate fish into large chunks. Arrange them in the pie dish, together with sautéed shrimps and scallops, and their juices.

7 Shell mussels and combine them with seafood in the pie dish.

8 Pour over sauce. Put dish aside to cool.

9 In the meantime, preheat oven to moderate (375°F Mark 5).

10 Roll two-thirds of pastry out to the same size as top of pie dish; fit it over fish and shellfish in dish, moistening and pinching edges to dish. Roll out remaining pastry; cut into strips about ½in wide and arrange over pastry in lattice fashion. Brush top of pie with beaten egg yolk and make vents in pastry to allow steam to escape.

11 Bake pie for thirty minutes, or until pastry crust is golden brown. Serve hot.

Fish and rice salad for a party

Serves 8–10
1 small cooked lobster, at least 1lb
4oz peeled prawns
1 small lemon sole

½lb turbot
4oz white button mushrooms
2 tablespoons lemon juice
1 cucumber
Salt
4 oz black olives
2 small green peppers
1 stalk celery
2 level tablespoons finely chopped parsley
Freshly ground black pepper

Fish stock (see step 3)
1 small carrot
1 small piece celery
4 sprigs parsley
Pinch of thyme
1 bay leaf
4 black peppercorns
¼ pint dry white wine

Dressing
8 fluid oz olive oil
8 tablespoons wine vinegar
2 tablespoons dry white wine
½ Spanish onion, very finely chopped
1 level tablespoon finely chopped chives
Salt and freshly ground black pepper

Saffron rice
1¼ pints chicken stock, made with 2 cubes
¼ level teaspoon saffron strands
6 tablespoons dry white wine
12oz long-grain rice
Salt and freshly ground black pepper

A large-scale and rather complicated salad, excellent for an
important buffet.

1 Remove meat from lobster (see p.132). Cut it into chunks where
possible and place it all in a bowl together with peeled prawns.

2 Skin and fillet sole (see p.103).

3 In a medium-sized pan, combine sole trimmings and a few pieces
   of lobster shell with stock ingredients. Add $\frac{3}{4}$ pint water. Bring
   slowly to the boil; cover and simmer for thirty minutes.

4 Meanwhile, prepare a dressing in another pan: beat olive oil, wine
   vinegar and dry white wine with a fork until mixture emulsifies;
   add finely chopped onion and chives, and season to taste with salt
   and freshly ground black pepper. Put aside, covered, until required.

5 Strain fish stock through a sieve lined with kitchen paper.

6 Pour 1in of strained stock into a deep, wide frying pan. Bring to
   the boil; remove from heat. Lay sole fillets in stock. After three
   minutes, turn them over and leave them for two to three minutes
   longer until just cooked.

7 Carefully remove sole fillets from stock. Cut into chunks and
   place in a warmed bowl. Cover and keep hot.

8 Cook turbot in the same stock for ten to twelve minutes over a low
   heat, turning once.

9 Remove turbot from pan; skin, bone and cut it into chunks. Place
   in another warmed bowl. Cover and keep hot.

10 Add 4 tablespoons hot fish stock to prepared dressing and mix well.
    Pour off $\frac{1}{4}$ pint dressing and reserve for later use. Heat remaining
    dressing gently until very warm.

11 Dress all the prepared fish and shellfish with warm dressing and
    leave to cool again, during which time they will absorb flavours.

12 Meanwhile, prepare saffron rice: make up chicken stock with
    2 cubes and $1\frac{1}{4}$ pints boiling water in a large pan. Pour 3 or 4
    tablespoons hot chicken stock over saffron strands in a cup and
    leave to soften and 'infuse' for ten minutes. Then mash saffron
    strands against sides of cup with a spoon to extract maximum
    colour and flavour.

13 Bring chicken stock to the boil with infused saffron and dry white wine. Gradually stir in rice and season to taste with salt and freshly ground black pepper. Reduce heat to a simmer; cover pan and cook gently, undisturbed, for twenty minutes, or until nearly all the liquid has been absorbed and rice is almost, but not quite, cooked. Remove pan from heat. Leave it on one side, still covered, to finish cooking and then gradually cool to lukewarm.

14 Meanwhile, prepare vegetables: wash or wipe mushrooms clean; trim stems and slice mushrooms thinly. Quickly toss them with lemon juice to prevent discolouration.

15 Peel cucumber and halve it lengthwise. Scoop out seeds with a teaspoon. Cut cucumber into $\frac{1}{4}$in dice. Place in a colander and toss with a little salt. Leave to drain.

16 Pit olives and slice them into rings. Put them in a bowl.

17 Halve, core and seed peppers. Cut them into strips $\frac{1}{8}$in wide and $1\frac{1}{2}$in long. Add to olives.

18 Cut celery into $\frac{1}{4}$in dice. Add to olives and peppers, and toss lightly.

19 When rice is lukewarm, carefully scoop it into a large mixing bowl. Drain off some of the dressing in which fish and shellfish were marinating and carefully, using a fork to avoid crushing grains, mix it into the rice.

20 Add drained mushrooms and cucumber, the olives, pepper strips, celery and finely chopped parsley, and continue to mix gently until thoroughly blended.

21 Finally, add fish and shellfish, together with remains of the dressing in which they were marinated. Fold them into the rice and vegetables, taking great care not to break the pieces.

22 Use some of the reserved dressing if salad is not moist enough. Correct seasoning and chill lightly until ready to serve.

Note: When coping with large quantities such as these, I find the best mixing tools are usually a pair of (clean) hands!

Cod

Greek skewered cod

Serves 6
1½lb cod (thick end of fillet)
4 tablespoons olive oil
2 tablespoons lemon juice
1 bay leaf, crumbled
Salt and freshly ground black pepper
4 firm, medium-sized tomatoes
3 small onions
Rice or shredded lettuce to serve

1 Combine olive oil, lemon juice, crumbled bay leaf and salt and
   freshly ground black pepper, to taste, in a small bowl to make
   basting sauce.

2 Cut cod into chunks (1–1½in square). You should have about
   thirty in all – any scrappy thin pieces should be rolled up into
   pieces the same size as chunks.

3 Slice tomatoes ¼in thick and onions ⅛in thick.

4 Thread six 8in or 9in metal skewers with alternate pieces of fish,
   tomato and onion slices, starting and ending with a chunk of fish,
   and dividing ingredients equally between skewers.

5 Line rack of grill pan with foil. Arrange skewers on it; brush with
   half the basting sauce and place under a preheated hot grill. Reduce
   heat to moderate and grill for four to five minutes.

6 Turn shewers; baste with remaining sauce and continue to grill
   for four to five minutes longer, or until fish flakes easily with a
   fork.

7 Serve immediately on a bed of rice or shredded lettuce, spooning
   some of the cooking juices over skewers.

Marinated cod steaks

Serves 4
4 slices fresh cod, about 1in thick
Marinade recipe 1 or 2
Butter
Onion
Well-flavoured fish stock (p.81), or canned clam juice
Salt and freshly ground black pepper
8 heart-shaped croûtons
4 slices grilled bacon
2 tablespoons finely chopped parsley

1 Marinate cod slices for at least four hours in marinade 1 or 2.

2 Place marinated cod steaks in (A) a well-buttered gratin dish with
   1 tablespoon finely chopped onion and 2 to 4 tablespoons fish
   stock or clam juice; season to taste with salt and freshly ground
   black pepper; place in double steamer; cover and steam until
   tender (fifteen to twenty minutes); or (B) in a saucepan on a bed of
   sliced onion; add $\frac{1}{4}$ pint fish stock, clam juice and just enough
   water to cover fish; season to taste with salt and freshly ground
   black pepper; cover pan, bring to a boil; lower heat and simmer
   gently for fifteen to twenty minutes, or until fish flakes easily with
   a fork.

3 To serve: place fish steaks on a heated serving dish; (A) pour over
   pan juices; garnish with croûtons, grilled bacon and finely chopped
   parsley, or (B) remove fish steaks to a heated serving dish and keep
   warm. Reduce fish stock to a quarter of its original quantity over
   a high heat; and strain a few tablespoons over fish. Garnish as above.

Cod marinade I

4 tablespoons olive oil
4 tablespoons dry white wine
2 level tablespoons finely chopped parsley
2 level tablespoons finely chopped onion
1 bay leaf, crumbled
Salt and freshly ground black pepper

1 Combine olive oil and dry white wine and flavour with finely
   chopped parsley and onion, crumbled bay leaf and salt and freshly
   ground black pepper, to taste.

2 Marinate fish in this mixture for at least two hours, turning fish
   from time to time.

Cod marinade II

2 tablespoons lemon juice
2 tablespoons Pernod
4 tablespoons olive oil
1 level teaspoon fennel seeds or chopped fennel leaves
Salt and freshly ground black pepper, to taste

1 Combine lemon juice and Pernod with olive oil and flavour with
   fennel seeds (or chopped fennel leaves). Add salt and freshly ground
   black pepper, to taste.

2 Marinate fish in this mixture for at least two hours, turning fish
   from time to time.

Italian poached cod with cold sauce

Serves 4–6
4–6 cod steaks
Juice of 1 lemon
Salt and freshly ground black pepper

Sauce
4 level tablespoons finely chopped Spanish onion
4 level tablespoons finely chopped parsley
2 cloves garlic, finely chopped
8 tablespoons olive oil
Juice of $\frac{1}{2}$ large lemon
Salt and freshly ground black pepper

1 Place cod steaks in a large frying pan; cover with cold water which
   you have flavoured with lemon juice and salt and freshly ground
   black pepper, to taste.

2 Bring to the boil; turn off heat and allow to steep in hot water for ten to twelve minutes. Remove steaks from liquid and place on a serving dish and allow to cool.

3 While cod steaks are steeping, combine sauce ingredients and chill.

4 When ready to serve, pour sauce over poached cod and serve.

Cod steaks in beer

Serves 8
1½ pints lager
1 carrot, sliced
1 Spanish onion, sliced
1 stalk celery, sliced
4 sprigs parsley
8 black peppercorns
5 cloves
1 bay leaf
8 thick cod steaks

Sauce
1oz butter
1oz flour
½ pint milk
½ pint fish liquor (see Step 3)
4 level tablespoons freshly grated Parmesan
4oz Gruyère, diced
2 egg yolks, lightly beaten
1 level tablespoon butter
4 level tablespoons double cream, whipped
Salt and freshly ground black pepper

This dish is also excellent if prepared in advance, then baked in a preheated moderate oven (375°F Mark 5) for twenty minutes before serving.

1 Pour lager into a deep frying pan large enough to take 4 cod steaks side by side. Add sliced vegetables, parsley sprigs,

peppercorns, cloves and the bay leaf; bring to the boil, cover and simmer for fifteen minutes.

2 Lay half the cod steaks in the simmering liquid and cook gently for fifteen to twenty minutes, or until they flake easily when tested with a fork, turning them once. Transfer cod steaks to a shallow baking dish or a heatproof serving dish, using a fish slice to avoid breaking them; keep hot. Cook remaining steaks in the same way.

3 Boil remaining cooking liquor briskly until reduced to about $\frac{1}{2}$ pint. Strain through a muslin-lined sieve.

4 To make sauce: melt butter in a heavy pan; blend in flour and cook over a low heat for two minutes, stirring constantly, to make a pale *roux*.

5 Gradually add milk and bring to the boil, stirring constantly until sauce is thick and smooth, and no longer tastes of flour.

6 Stir in strained fish liquor; add freshly grated Parmesan, diced Gruyère and lightly beaten egg yolks, and cook over a very low heat, beating vigorously with a wooden spoon until sauce is smooth and hot again, and taking care not to let it boil, or egg yolks may curdle.

7 Stir in butter and whipped cream, and season to taste with salt and freshly ground black pepper.

8 Pour sauce over cod steaks. Slip under a hot grill until top is golden brown and bubbling. Serve immediately.

Haddock

Fresh haddock with lemon butter

Serves 4
4 fillets fresh haddock
Lemon juice
Salt and freshly ground black pepper

Salted water
Sprigs of fresh parsley
Boiled potatoes
¼lb butter, melted

1 Cut fillets into manageable portions; season with lemon juice,
salt and freshly ground black pepper, and poach them gently in
simmering salted water for about twenty minutes, or until fish
flakes easily with a fork.

2 Transfer haddock fillets to a heated serving dish and garnish with
sprigs of parsley and boiled potatoes.

3 Serve with melted butter seasoned to taste with lemon juice, salt
and freshly ground black pepper.

Baked fresh haddock

Serves 4–6
1 small fresh haddock (about 3lb)
¼ Spanish onion, finely chopped
8 button mushrooms, finely chopped
Butter
2 tablespoons finely chopped parsley
Salt and freshly ground black pepper
¼ pint double cream or dry white wine

1 Preheat oven to moderate (375°F Mark 5).

2 Sauté finely chopped onion and mushrooms in 2 tablespoons butter
until onion is transparent.

3 Wipe cleaned and scaled fish well with a damp cloth and place it in
a well-buttered shallow baking dish in which you have sprinkled
half the onion and mushroom mixture.

4 Cover fish with remaining onions and mushrooms; season with
finely chopped parsley, and salt and freshly ground black pepper,
to taste, and add ¼ pint double cream or dry white wine.

5 Bake in a moderate oven (375°F Mark 5) until fish flakes easily with a fork.

6 Serve immediately in the baking dish.

Smoked haddock mousse

Serves 4
1lb smoked haddock
$\frac{1}{2}$ pint milk
Oil for mould
3oz butter
3oz flour
$\frac{1}{4}$ pint single cream
Salt and freshly ground black pepper
3 egg yolks
Juice of $\frac{1}{2}$ lemon
2 level tablespoons finely chopped parsley
Pinch of cayenne

The sad thing about smoked haddock is its cheapness – otherwise it would certainly be treated with greater respect than it is today.

1 Soak fish in cold water for about one hour to remove excess salt. Then drain; place in a saucepan and cover with the milk and $\frac{1}{2}$ pint water. Bring to the boil, simmer for two to three minutes, and put aside.

2 Preheat oven to moderate (350°F Mark 4).

3 Brush a plain, $1\frac{1}{2}$ pint ring mould generously with oil.

4 In a heavy pan, melt butter; add flour and stir together over a low heat for two minutes to make a pale *roux*.

5 Drain fish. Add cooking liquor to *roux* gradually, stirring vigorously to make a smooth sauce. Cook over a moderate heat, stirring, until sauce comes to the boil, and simmer for four to five minutes longer. Then remove pan from heat; stir in cream and season generously with salt and freshly ground black pepper.

6 Remove all bones and skin from haddock, and blend fish to a purée in an electric blender together with ½ pint of the sauce and the egg yolks. Taste purée for seasoning. It should be rather strongly flavoured.

7 When haddock mixture is quite smooth, spoon it into mould and level off top. Place mould in a deep baking dish with hot water to come three-quarters of the way up sides.

8 Bake mousse until firm, thirty to thirty-five minutes.

9 Stir lemon juice, finely chopped parsley and a pinch of cayenne into remaining sauce, and reheat gently.

10 When ready to serve: carefully unmould mousse on to a flat heated serving dish. Spoon hot sauce over sides and centre of mousse, and serve immediately.

Herrings

Grilled herrings with mustard

Serves 4
4 fresh herrings
2 tablespoons flour
Salt and freshly ground black pepper
Olive oil
French mustard
Freshly grated breadcrumbs
4 tablespoons melted butter
Boiled new potatoes

1 Clean and scale herrings, taking care not to break the delicate skin underneath; cut off heads; wash and dry carefully.

2 Make three shallow incisions on sides of each fish with a sharp knife.

3 Dip herrings in seasoned flour; brush them with olive oil and grill on a well-oiled baking sheet for three to four minutes on each side.

4 Arrange herrings in a shallow ovenproof gratin dish; brush them liberally with French mustard; sprinkle with freshly grated breadcrumbs and melted butter, and put in a very hot oven (475°F Mark 9) for five minutes. Serve in the gratin dish with boiled new potatoes.

Baked herrings

Serves 4
4 fresh herrings
Butter
Fresh breadcrumbs
Finely chopped parsley
Salt and freshly ground black pepper
Lemon wedges

1 Clean and scale herrings, taking care not to break the delicate skin underneath; cut off heads; wash and dry carefully.

2 Remove roes; detach skin and pound roes with an equal amount of softened butter. Force mixture through a fine sieve; mix in 2–4 tablespoons fresh breadcrumbs, flavour with finely chopped parsley, and season to taste with salt and freshly ground black pepper.

3 Slit herrings down backbone with a sharp knife and remove backbone carefully, snipping both ends free with kitchen scissors.

4 Stuff herrings with roe mixture and place fish in a lightly buttered shallow ovenproof dish. Sprinkle lightly with breadcrumbs, finely chopped parsley and melted butter.

5 Cover fish with buttered paper and bake in a moderately hot oven (400°F Mark 6) for fifteen to twenty minutes, or until cooked through. Just before serving, brown under grill. Serve with lemon wedges.

Salmon

Sautéed salmon steaks

Serves 4
4 fresh salmon steaks
Flour
4 tablespoons butter
¼ pint dry white wine
Bay leaf
Salt
White pepper
Pinch of celery seed
2 tablespoons finely chopped parsley

1 Choose centre cuts of salmon about ¾in thick.

2 Rub steaks well on both sides with flour.

3 Melt butter in a heavy frying pan or shallow heatproof casserole, and when hot, sauté steaks lightly.

4 When steaks are light brown, add white wine and seasonings.

5 Cover and simmer, with frequent basting, on top of stove until cooked (about thirty minutes). When salmon is cooked, sprinkle with finely chopped parsley and serve.

Grilled salmon steaks

Serves 4
4 large salmon steaks
Salt and freshly ground black pepper
4 tablespoons melted butter
Lemon wedges

Lemon and parsley butter
¼lb slightly softened butter
2 tablespoons finely chopped parsley

Lemon juice
Salt and freshly ground black pepper

1 Season both sides of salmon steaks to taste with salt and freshly ground black pepper, and leave to stand at room temperature for fifteen minutes.

2 Place steaks on a buttered, preheated baking sheet; brush with 2 tablespoons melted butter and grill for three to five minutes about 3in from heat.

3 Turn steaks, brush with remaining butter and grill until fish flakes easily with a fork (three to five minutes).

4 Serve with lemon and parsley butter and lemon wedges.

5 *To make lemon and parsley butter*: pound slightly softened butter in a mortar with finely chopped parsley, and lemon juice, salt and freshly ground black pepper to taste.

Peppered salmon steaks

Serves 4
4 salmon steaks, $\frac{3}{4}$in thick
2 level tablespoons coarsely crushed black pepper
Salt
4 tablespoons melted butter
Juice of $\frac{1}{2}$ lemon
2 level tablespoons finely chopped parsley

1 Press crushed peppercorns into the flesh of the salmon steaks with the heel of your hand and sprinkle with salt to taste.

2 Brush steaks with melted butter and sprinkle with lemon juice.

3 Grill steaks about 4in from the heat for eight to ten minutes on each side, brushing with melted butter when you turn them over.

4 When steaks are done, place them on a heated serving dish and garnish with finely chopped parsley.

Salmon brochettes

Serves 4
2–3 fresh salmon steaks (about 1½in thick)
6 tablespoons olive oil
2 tablespoons lemon juice
½ Spanish onion, finely chopped
4 tablespoons finely chopped parsley
Salt and freshly ground black pepper
4 small onions, sliced
4 tomatoes, sliced
Lemon juice

1 Cut fresh salmon steaks into 1in cubes and marinate for at least two hours in olive oil, lemon juice, finely chopped onion and parsley, and salt and freshly ground black pepper, to taste.

2 Place fish cubes on a skewer alternately with a slice of onion, a slice of tomato.

3 Grill over charcoal or under the grill, turning frequently and basting from time to time with marinade sauce.

4 To serve: remove cooked fish from skewer on to serving plate and sprinkle with lemon juice.

Sole

Sole bonne femme

Serves 4
4 soles, about 12oz each
1 lemon
4 level tablespoons finely chopped parsley
Salt and freshly ground black pepper
About 4oz butter
8oz button mushrooms, sliced
½ pint dry white wine
1 level tablespoon flour

¼ pint double cream
1 egg yolk

1 Clean soles. Ask the fishmonger to remove the black skin, or do it yourself as follows: make a small incision above the tail and pare away enough skin to give you a good grip; then pull the skin sharply towards the head. Lay soles, skinned side up, on a board.

2 Cut lemon in half; cut one half into thin slices for garnish. Keep remaining half to season fish.

3 Preheat oven to moderate (375°F Mark 5).

4 Make an incision in each fish down the length of the backbone on the skinned side and slide a thin knife blade under each side. Lift up fillets carefully and sprinkle the pockets with finely chopped parsley (using half of the total amount), a few drops of lemon juice, and salt and freshly ground black pepper, to taste.

5 Butter an ovenproof baking dish large enough to take all the fish in one layer. Sprinkle dish with sliced mushrooms; arrange fish on top and dust with remaining chopped parsley. Add dry white wine and just enough water to cover soles.

6 Cover dish with a buttered paper; bring to simmering point on top of the stove and transfer to the oven. Bake for about twenty minutes, or until fish flakes easily with a fork.

7 When fish are cooked, transfer them to a heated serving dish and keep warm while you finish sauce.

8 Reduce cooking liquor to about half by boiling it briskly over a high heat.

9 Make a *beurre manié* by mashing 1 level tablespoon each butter and flour together to a smooth paste. Thin it down with a little of the reduced stock; then pour back into the pan; bring to the boil, stirring constantly, and simmer for two to three minutes to cook flour and thicken sauce.

10 Add cream; remove from heat and beat in the egg yolk and the remaining butter in small pieces.

11 When sauce is smooth and shiny, pour over soles. Garnish dish with lemon slices and serve immediately.

Sole with crevettes

Serves 4
2 large sole, about 1¾lb each
Salt and freshly ground black pepper
Lemon juice
8 crevettes, with shells, about 8oz
¼ pint dry white wine
Butter

Fish stock
Fish trimmings (see Step 1)
Salt
1 carrot, chopped
1 leek, white part only, chopped
Small strip of lemon zest
6 black peppercorns
3–4 sprigs parsley
1 bay leaf

Sauce
2 level tablespoons butter
2 level tablespoons flour
Reduced fish liquor (see Step 9)
¼ pint double cream
2 egg yolks
2–3 teaspoons Pernod
Lemon juice
1 level tablespoon finely chopped parsley
Salt and freshly ground black pepper

1 Have your fishmonger skin and fillet sole, and ask him to let you have the trimmings from them.

2 To make fish stock: place sole trimmings in a pan with a pint of cold water. Add a little salt; bring slowly to the boil; skim and add remaining ingredients. Simmer gently, covered, for thirty minutes; then remove lid and continue to simmer for a further thirty minutes. Strain stock through a fine sieve into a measuring jug.

3 Season fillets on both sides with salt and freshly ground black pepper. Lay fillets on a board skin side (or with the side that *was* skinned) upwards. Sprinkle with lemon juice.

4 Shell crevettes; remove heads but leave on the two fins right at the end of the tail. Reserve shells and trimmings.

5 Preheat oven to moderate (375°F Mark 5).

6 Place a crevette at the wider end of each fillet and roll up. The tail of the crevette should stick out at one end.

7 Arrange rolled sole fillets tightly side by side in a deep, heatproof casserole or baking dish. The tails of the crevettes will stick up in the air. Pour over wine. Cover casserole with a buttered paper.

8 Place casserole over a moderately low heat; bring to simmering point; transfer to the oven and bake for ten minutes, or until fish flakes easily with a fork, but is not overcooked.

9 Carefully drain off liquor from casserole into the measuring jug. Keep sole hot. Note the quantity of fish stock and wine; pour into a pan; add shells, heads, etc. from crevettes and boil rapidly until reduced to $\frac{1}{2}$ pint.

10 To make sauce: in the top of a double saucepan, melt butter over direct heat. Blend in flour with a wooden spoon and stir over a low heat for two to three minutes to make a pale *roux*.

11 Gradually add reduced fish liquor, stirring vigorously to prevent lumps forming; bring to the boil and simmer for two or three minutes, stirring. Remove from heat.

12 Stir in cream and beat in egg yolks. Fit top of pan over base
    containing simmering water and cook gently, stirring, until sauce
    has thickened again. Take care not to let it boil, or egg yolks may
    curdle.

13 Flavour sauce with Pernod and a few drops of lemon juice; stir in
    finely chopped parsley and correct seasoning if necessary Spoon
    sauce over rolled fillets of sole, avoiding crevette tails, and serve.

Pain de sole

Serves 8
1¼lb fillets of sole (weight after filleting)
3 egg whites
Salt, freshly ground black pepper and cayenne
¾ pint double cream
6oz fresh white breadcrumbs
3 eggs
4 level tablespoons finely chopped parsley
2 level tablespoons finely chopped tarragon
1 level tablespoon finely chopped chives
Fresh fennel or tarragon sprigs
Thin strips of pork fat
Mousseline-Hollandaise sauce (p.108)

1 *Prepare a fish mousseline*: set aside 4 good-sized fillets of sole and
   put remainder of fish through a mincer. Stir in 2 unbeaten egg
   whites; then rub fish mixture through a fine sieve into a bowl.

2 Set bowl in a larger bowl containing ice cubes. Work mixture with
   a spatula, adding a little salt, which will make fish stiffen and
   change its consistency, freshly ground black pepper and a pinch of
   cayenne, to taste. When fish 'stiffens', add ½ pint cream, a little at a
   time, working paste vigorously with the spatula. Cover bowl and
   leave mousseline at the bottom of the refrigerator until needed.

3 *Prepare herb forcemeat*: put fresh breadcrumbs in a bowl. Beat
   whole eggs lightly and whisk in remaining cream until it forms
   soft peaks. Add this to breadcrumbs, together with finely chopped

herbs, and mix well. Season to taste with salt and freshly ground black pepper.

4 Beat remaining egg white until foamy.

5 Season reserved fillets of sole with salt and freshly ground black pepper.

6 Select a rectangular 4 pint terrine and arrange 2 or 3 sprigs of fresh fennel or tarragon decoratively on the base. Line base and sides of terrine with long, thin strips of pork fat, making sure they overlap at both ends so that they can be folded over the top of the terrine when it is full.

7 To assemble the *pain de sole*: spread base and sides of terrine with an even layer of mousseline, using about two-thirds of the total amount. Brush with lightly beaten egg white and place 2 whole fillets of sole on this bed. Brush fillets with more egg white and cover with half of the forcemeat. Brush with egg white again; lay remaining fillets of sole on top and brush them also. Cover fillets with remaining forcemeat; brush with egg white; then fill dish with remaining mousseline.

8 Fold over overhanging strips of pork fat so that top of mousseline is completely covered. If not to be cooked immediately, cover with a lid and place in refrigerator. Remove terrine from refrigerator two hours before you intend to put it into the oven.

9 Preheat oven to very slow (300°F Mark 2).

10 Place covered terrine in a pan with boiling water to come a third of the way up its sides. Bake for one and three-quarters to two hours, or until a sharp skewer pushed through the centre and held there for a few seconds feels hot on the palm of your hand.

11 Turn *pain de sole* out on to a heated serving dish and serve warm, cut in thick slices, accompanied by a Mousseline-Hollandaise sauce (see p.108).

Mousseline-Hollandaise sauce

Serves 8
Lemon juice
Salt and white pepper
¼lb softened butter
4 egg yolks
4–6 tablespoons whipped cream

1 Combine 1 teaspoon lemon juice with a tablespoon of cold water, and salt and white pepper, to taste, in the top of a double saucepan.

2 Divide softened butter into four equal pieces.

3 Add egg yolks and a quarter of the butter to the liquid in the saucepan, and stir mixture rapidly and constantly with a wire whisk over hot but not boiling water until butter has melted and mixture begins to thicken.

4 Add the second piece of butter and continue whisking. As the mixture thickens and the second piece of butter melts, add the third piece of butter, stirring from the bottom of the pan until it has melted. Be careful not to allow water over which sauce is cooking to boil at any time. Add rest of butter, beating until it melts and is incorporated into the sauce.

5 Now remove top part of pan from the heat and continue to beat sauce for two to three minutes longer.

6 Replace pan over hot but not boiling water for two minutes more, beating constantly. By this time the emulsion should have formed and your sauce will be rich and creamy. 'Finish' sauce with a few drops of lemon juice, to taste; strain.

7 Just before serving, fold in whipped cream and season to taste with a little more salt or white pepper if necessary.

Note: If at any stage in the operation the mixture should curdle beat in 1 or 2 tablespoons cold water to rebind the emulsion.

Trout

Trout à la Grecque

Serves 2–4
2 trout, about 1lb each
1½ chicken stock cubes
½lb carrots
½lb baby turnips
½lb potatoes
¼lb frozen peas
Twists of lemon, to garnish

Dressing
6 tablespoons olive oil
1 tablespoon dry white wine
2–3 teaspoons lemon juice
1 level tablespoon finely chopped parsley
1 level tablespoon finely chopped chives (optional)
1 level teaspoon grated onion
Salt and freshly ground black pepper
6–8 fennel seeds

Timing is all-important to the success of this attractive dish.

1 Select a heavy, oval, heatproof casserole long enough to hold trout comfortably without bending them. In it dissolve stock cubes in 1½ pints water.

2 Peel carrots, turnips and potatoes. Cut them into ¼in dice. Place potatoes in a bowl of cold water.

3 Bring chicken stock to the boil. Add diced carrots and turnips; lower heat to simmering point; cover and cook gently for five minutes.

4 Drain potatoes thoroughly and add them to the casserole, together with frozen peas. Bring to the boil again; lower heat to simmering point; cover and continue to simmer for a further four minutes. Keep testing potatoes towards the end of this time: they should be soft, but on no account overcooked.

5 Submerge trout in stock and vegetables; bring rapidly to the boil; then cover casserole again; remove from heat and allow trout to cook from the heat of the pan itself for ten minutes. Then plunge casserole into cold water to cool contents quickly and prevent it cooking any further.

6 When casserole is quite cold, chill until ready to serve. It may be left overnight if more convenient.

7 Just before serving, combine dressing ingredients in a bowl and beat with a fork until emulsified. Dressing should be quite highly flavoured and seasoned.

8 To serve: remove trout from casserole, taking care not to break them, and drain on absorbent paper.

9 Drain vegetables; place them in a bowl and toss gently with 4 tablespoons dressing. Taste and correct seasoning if necessary.

10 Arrange trout in the centre of a large oval dish. Surround with dressed vegetables. Spoon more of the dressing over the fish and garnish with twists of lemon. Serve very cold, accompanied by remaining dressing.

Serve ½ fish per person as an appetiser; a whole one as the main course of a light summer lunch.

Trout with almonds

Serves 4–6
4–6 fresh trout, cleaned
Salt and freshly ground black pepper
Milk
Flour
¼lb butter
1 tablespoon olive oil
4–6 level tablespoons flaked almonds
Juice of ½ lemon
2–4 level tablespoons finely chopped parsley

1 Season cleaned trout with salt and a little freshly ground black pepper. Dip them in milk and then in flour, shaking off excess.

2 In a large frying pan (or two pans) which will take the trout in one layer, melt half the butter with olive oil. Sauté fish until they are golden brown on both sides and flesh flakes easily with a fork, four to five minutes on each side. Remove to a heated platter.

3 Drain fat from pan and add remaining butter. When it has melted, add flaked almonds and sauté, shaking pan continuously, until almonds are golden brown. Take care over this, as they burn easily. Sprinkle with lemon juice and finely chopped parsley.

4 Pour buttery sauce and almonds over trout, and serve immediately.

Turbot

Blanquette of turbot

Serves 8 as an entrée, garnished with crescents of puff pastry, or 4–6 as a main course served with rice
2lb turbot
5oz butter
$\frac{1}{2}$ pint dry white wine
24 button onions
2 level tablespoons castor sugar
Salt and freshly ground black pepper
8oz tight white button mushrooms
1oz flour
1 egg yolk
$\frac{1}{3}$ pint (7 fluid oz) double cream
Lemon juice
3–4 level tablespoons finely chopped parsley
Crescents of puff pastry or plain-boiled rice, to serve

Stock
4 leeks, white parts only, thinly sliced
4 carrots, thinly sliced
1oz butter

Fish heads and trimmings
2 onions, each stuck with 1 clove
Bouquet garni (4 sprigs parsley, 2 sprigs thyme, 1 large bay
    leaf)
Salt and freshly ground black pepper

Turbot is ideal for a blanquette as it is less likely to disintegrate during cooking than a fish like cod or haddock. However, you should be just as careful not to overcook it, leaving it on the firm side if anything.

1 First prepare stock: in a large pan or casserole, sauté thinly sliced leeks and carrots in butter until lightly coloured. Cover with 3 pints water and add fish heads and trimmings (ask your fishmonger for these when you buy the fish), the onions stuck with cloves, bouquet garni, and a light seasoning of salt and freshly ground black pepper. Bring to the boil and simmer until reduced by half, about twenty minutes. Strain stock through a fine sieve and keep hot.

2 Cut turbot in 24 even-sized cubes.

3 Heat 2oz butter in a heavy pan until lightly coloured and sauté turbot cubes until pale golden colour on all sides, taking great care not to break them.

4 Add strained stock and dry white wine; bring to the boil over a moderate heat and simmer very, very gently until turbot is cooked through but still firm, ten to fifteen minutes.

5 Meanwhile, put button onions in a small pan and cover with water. Add 1oz butter, the sugar, and salt and freshly ground black pepper, to taste. Bring to the boil and simmer until liquid has boiled away and onions are lightly caramelised, shaking pan towards the end to colour them evenly. Keep hot.

6 Wipe mushrooms and trim stems; leave them whole if they are very small, halve or quarter them if larger. Put mushrooms in a small pan with 1oz butter and toss over a gentle heat until softened. Keep hot.

7 When turbot is ready, remove from pan with a slotted spoon and
  keep hot. Simmer cooking liquor until reduced to 1 pint.

8 Melt remaining 1oz butter in a large pan or casserole; add flour
  and stir over a low heat for two minutes to make a pale *roux*.
  Gradually stir in reduced cooking liquor, beating vigorously to
  prevent lumps forming, and bring to the boil, stirring constantly;
  then lower heat and simmer for ten minutes, stirring occasionally.
  Remove from heat.

9 Beat egg yolk with cream and lemon juice, to taste. Add to sauce;
  mix well; return pan to a very low heat and continue to stir until
  sauce thickens, taking care not to let it come to the boil, or egg
  yolk may curdle.

10 Fold in turbot and mushrooms; correct seasoning, adding more
   salt, freshly ground black pepper or lemon juice if necessary, and
   heat through gently.

11 Turn blanquette into a large, heated serving dish. Sprinkle with
   finely chopped parsley and garnish with glazed button onions.
   Serve very hot, garnished with crescents of puff pastry or
   rice.

Halibut

Poached halibut Hollandaise

Serves 4
4 halibut steaks, 1½in thick
Juice of 1 lemon
½ onion, finely sliced
1 bay leaf
6 peppercorns
Salt
Fresh watercress or parsley sprigs
2 lemons, cut into wedges

Hollandaise sauce
(Makes about ½ pint)
Lemon juice
Salt and white pepper

8oz softened butter
4 egg yolks

1 Place halibut steaks in a large frying-pan. Add cold water to just cover steaks and season with lemon juice, sliced onion, bay leaf, peppercorns and salt, to taste.

2 Bring to the boil; reduce heat and simmer for ten minutes or until fish flakes easily with a fork. Do not overcook.

3 Drain steaks thoroughly on a clean kitchen towel.

4 Place steaks on a hot serving dish and spoon a little Hollandaise sauce over each steak. Serve remaining sauce in a sauce boat.

5 Garnish dish with sprigs of fresh watercress or parsley, and lemon wedges.

6 *To make Hollandaise sauce*: in the top of a double saucepan, combine a teaspoon of lemon juice with a tablespoon of cold water and a pinch each of salt and white pepper.

7 Put softened butter on a plate and divide into 4 pieces of equal size.

8 Add egg yolks and 1 piece butter to the liquid in the pan and place over hot water. Stir rapidly with a wire whisk for about five minutes, or until butter has melted completely and mixture begins to thicken, making sure water underneath never comes to the boil.

9 Incorporate remaining pieces of butter one at a time, whisking vigorously and stirring from the bottom of the pan.

10 When sauce is thick and emulsified, beat for two to three minutes longer; then correct seasoning, adding more salt, white pepper or lemon juice to taste. Strain, if necessary, and serve.

Scallops

One of my favourite kinds of shellfish – and one still within the means of most mortals – scallops taste as good as they look, with their creamy round lobes and bright red corals resting on the half-shell.

If you are ever lucky enough to find the 'miniature' variety (sadly, most of these seem destined to be exported to North America), these are even sweeter in flavour.

When buying scallops in the shell, make sure they are tightly closed. This indicates that they are still alive and safe to eat.

To open a scallop

Slip a short, stubby knife blade between the shells as near to the hinge as you can get. This is to be found at the centre of the straight back edge, where the ribbing on the shells converges to a point. Cut through the hinge level with the shell. This will release the tension and the shell can be prised apart quite easily.

To clean a scallop

1 Remove scallop from half-shell. Discard the black piece sticking to it and the little tube trailing from the end.

2 Wash scallop carefully under cold running water to remove every trace of sand. The 'beard' is either retained, in which case make sure it is free of sand, or discarded, as you prefer.

Basic poached scallops

Serves 4–6
8–12 large scallops, with corals
$\frac{1}{2}$ small onion, chopped
Bouquet garni (2 sprigs parsley, 1 sprig thyme, 1 small bay leaf)
$\frac{1}{2}$ pint dry white wine
Salt and freshly ground black pepper

1 Rinse scallops if necessary. Trim off any ragged edges, but leave red 'corals' attached. They are a delicacy.

2 Place scallops in a small pan. Add chopped onion, bouquet garni, dry white wine and, if necessary, a little cold water so that scallops are just covered with liquid. Season lightly with salt and freshly ground black pepper.

3 Bring scallops to simmering point over a moderately low heat, and poach gently for five minutes. (If scallops are small, they will be ready even sooner.) Take great care not to overcook them or their delicate texture will be ruined and they will turn tough and fibrous.

4 As soon as scallops are ready, lift them out of the pan with a slotted spoon. Use as required. Large scallops are usually sliced thickly in two or three. Small ones may be left whole, or halved.

Some variations on the basic poached scallops theme

Deep-fried scallops and bacon

Serves 4–6
8–12 large scallops, with corals
$\frac{1}{2}$ small onion, chopped
Bouquet garni (2 sprigs parsley, 1 sprig thyme, 1 small bay leaf)
$\frac{1}{2}$ pint dry white wine
Salt and freshly ground black pepper
2 eggs, beaten
Milk
Cayenne
Fresh breadcrumbs
$\frac{1}{4}$lb butter
$\frac{1}{4}$ pint olive oil
6 slices bacon
Lemon wedges

Steps 1–4 as in basic recipe on p.115.

5 Combine beaten eggs and a little milk in a flat bowl, and season to taste with salt, freshly ground black pepper and cayenne.

6 Dip sliced poached scallops (or whole if they are small) in egg mixture and then in fresh breadcrumbs and allow to set in the refrigerator for at least one hour before cooking.

7 When ready to serve, melt butter in a large, thick-bottomed frying pan; add olive oil; bring to frying temperature and cook bacon slices until crisp. Remove and keep warm.

8 Add prepared scallops and cook in hot fat until they are golden brown. Serve immediately accompanied by crisp bacon and wedges of lemon.

Coquilles Saint-Jacques au gratin

Serves 4–6
8–12 large scallops with corals
½ small onion, chopped
Bouquet garni (2 sprigs parsley, 1 sprig thyme, 1 small bay leaf)
½ pint dry white wine
Salt and freshly ground black pepper
6oz finely chopped button mushrooms
2oz finely chopped Spanish onion
Butter
2 level tablespoons finely chopped parsley
4 tablespoons reduced *fish velouté sauce* (p.118)
Freshly grated Parmesan
Fresh breadcrumbs

Steps 1–4 as in basic recipe (p.115).

5 Simmer finely chopped button mushrooms and finely chopped Spanish onion in 4 level tablespoons butter until soft. Reserve.

6 Add finely chopped parsley and reduced *fish velouté sauce* to mushroom and onion mixture.

Note: I sometimes just add 4 tablespoons reduced fish stock which I have thickened with ½ level teaspoon each flour and butter mashed to a smooth paste.

7 Toss poached, sliced scallops in this mixture and fill cleaned scallop shells or individual heatproof dishes with this mixture.

8 Sprinkle with a little freshly grated Parmesan and fresh breadcrumbs; sprinkle with a little melted butter and put under the grill until bubbling hot and golden brown.

Fish velouté sauce

Makes ⅔ pint
2 level tablespoons butter
2 level tablespoons flour
1 pint boiling fish stock or canned clam juice
Salt and white pepper
Lemon juice

1 Melt butter in the top of a double saucepan; add flour and cook for a few minutes to form a pale *roux*.

2 Add boiling stock (or canned clam juice) and salt and pepper, to taste, and cook, stirring vigorously with a whisk until well blended.

3 Reduce heat and simmer gently, stirring occasionally and skimming from time to time until the sauce is reduced to two-thirds of the original quantity and is thick but light and creamy.

4 Flavour with lemon juice, to taste and strain through a fine sieve.

Note: *Fish velouté* – makes an excellent sauce on its own when a little double cream and 1 or 2 egg yolks are added.

Coquilles Saint-Jacques à la Bretonne

Serves 4
8 large scallops, fresh or frozen
¼ pint dry white wine
Salt and freshly ground black pepper
3oz stale white breadcrumbs
6 tablespoons milk
1 Spanish onion, finely chopped

1 shallot, finely chopped
3oz butter
1 tablespoon cognac
1 clove garlic, crushed
2 level tablespoons finely chopped parsley
1 level tablespoon flour
4 level tablespoons fine white breadcrumbs

An excellent hot *hors-d'œuvre* which can be prepared in advance and slipped under a hot grill to reheat and brown the top just before serving.

1 If fresh scallops are available, shell and clean them, following directions. The 'beard' should be retained – in Brittany this is served with the rest of the scallops and it is delicious. Wash scallops carefully in running water to remove every trace of sand.

2 If using frozen scallops, allow them to thaw completely.

3 Cut each scallop into large dice, leaving the coral in one piece.

4 Place scallops, corals and 'beards' in a small pan; add wine, and salt and freshly ground black pepper to taste, and poach very gently for about five minutes. Drain, reserving poaching liquor, and keep hot.

5 Put stale breadcrumbs in a bowl and sprinkle with milk.

6 In a small pan, sauté finely chopped onion and shallot in 2oz butter until soft and golden. Add scallops and continue to sauté for two to three minutes, stirring gently with a wooden spoon. Stir in cognac.

7 Add soaked breadcrumbs, together with crushed garlic and finely chopped parsley, and simmer for two to three minutes longer, stirring constantly.

8 Sprinkle with flour and moisten with reserved poaching liquor. Season to taste with salt and freshly ground black pepper, and allow to simmer gently for a final five or six minutes, stirring. The sauce should have the consistency of a Béchamel.

9 Scrub 4 empty scallop shells clean. (If preparing the dish with frozen scallops, use individual heatproof ramekins instead.) Divide scallops and sauce equally between them; sprinkle with fresh breadcrumbs and dot with remaining butter.

10 Just before serving, place shells or dishes under a preheated, very hot grill until tops are golden brown and bubbling.

Scallop brochettes

Serves 6
6 large scallops, with corals
$\frac{1}{2}$ pint dry white wine
3 level tablespoons finely chopped onion
2–3 sprigs parsley
1 sprig thyme or $\frac{1}{4}$ level teaspoon dried thyme
1 bay leaf
Salt and freshly ground black pepper
6oz bacon in one piece
4–5 level tablespoons flour
4–6 level tablespoons fine dry white breadcrumbs
1 egg
Oil for deep-frying
Hollandaise sauce (p.114, Steps 6 to 10), to serve

1 Wipe scallops; put them in a small pan and add white wine, finely chopped onion and herbs. Season to taste with salt and freshly ground black pepper. Bring to a gentle boil; lower heat and simmer for about five minutes, or until scallops are just cooked. Remove from heat.

2 Take scallops out of pan with a slotted spoon. Separate corals and cut them in two across the width. Slice white parts in three. Drop scallops and corals back into cooking liquor and leave to cool.

3 Meanwhile, cut bacon into 12 batons, each about 1in long and $\frac{1}{2}$in thick. Put them in a small pan; bring to the boil; simmer for two minutes and drain. Cool.

4 Sift flour on to one flat plate, and scatter breadcrumbs over another

120

one. In a shallow dish, beat egg lightly with a tablespoon of cold water.

5 When scallops and bacon are cool, drain them and dry them thoroughly with absorbent paper.

6 Dust scallop slices, corals and bacon batons with flour; dip each piece in beaten egg, allowing excess to drain off, and coat with breadcrumbs, making sure they cover the entire surface.

7 Thread ingredients on to six 6in skewers, assembling each one as follows: 1 slice scallop, 1 baton bacon, 1 piece coral, scallop, bacon, coral and scallop. Chill skewers until ready to fry them.

8 Heat a pan of oil for deep-frying to 400°F, or until a cube of bread browns in forty-five seconds.

9 Plunge skewers (about three at a time) into hot oil and deep-fry for two minutes, or until nicely browned. Drain on paper towels. Allow fat to reach 400°F again before frying remaining skewers.

10 Serve immediately with Hollandaise sauce.

Crab

Found both in salt and fresh water, crabs are available more or less all the year round, but are at their best from May to August. Crabs contain less meat for their size than lobsters, but the meat is a good deal sweeter and many people prefer its delicate flavour.

To choose a crab

Choose heavy crabs of medium size; the light ones tend to be watery. The male crab – recognised by its larger claws – is considered better than the hen, but this is far less important than the weight test.

To shell a cooked crab

You will need a cleaver or a heavy knife with a strong blade, plus a wooden mallet or rolling pin and a metal skewer or wooden toothpicks, a board on which to work, and two bowls.

1 Lay crab on its back with its tail flap nearest you and the large claws at the side farthest away from you. If the crab is a small one, you will probably be able to separate the chest section from the hard carapace by placing your thumbs under the tail flap and pushing upwards. If it is a mature crab, it will be easier to prise the two sections apart with the tip of your cleaver, pushing it down between carapace and chest section at the tail. Put aside the chest section with claws and legs attached.

2 Take the carapace; turn it around and remove the mouthpiece together with the stomach, which resembles a crumpled greaseproof bag. Lift out transparent membranes and any white gills which may have come loose from the chest section. These go under the dubious name of 'dead men's fingers'.

3 Scoop out the creamy meat into a bowl. If you are careful, you will be able to keep it in reasonably large pieces. Where it joins the shell the meat will have a reddish hue, changing to greenish grey towards the centre. All of this is edible.

4 Take the chest section. Break off claws and legs close to body.

5 *Legs*: in a small crab, the only part of the legs worth shelling is the first joint or thigh. Separate this from the remaining sections by bending it back *against* the joint so that the cartilage is drawn out of it as the two come apart. When all the thigh pieces have been separated, lay them flat on your board, one at a time, and give them a good whack with the side of your cleaver. Pick off cracked shell and place pieces of meat in the second bowl. If the crab is a large one, it will pay you to take the remaining leg joints, separating them as before so that the cartilage is drawn out before you crush the shells and remove meat.

6 *Claws*: pull the smaller part of each claw back on itself so that it comes away with the cartilage from the larger claw. Then divide

claw into joints in the same way. Crack each piece of claw by hitting it smartly with the side of your cleaver or the wooden mallet. Pick off shell, keeping pieces of meat as large as possible, and making sure they are quite free of shell splinters. Put meat in the second bowl.

7 Now clean your board and take the chest section. Peel off all the feathery white gills attached to the underside. If it is a small crab, all you can do is dig as much meat as possible out of the holes left by the legs and claws, and then from the centre, using a skewer or toothpick. If you are dealing with a large crab, chop the chest section in four with your cleaver to get at the quite considerable amount of meat nestling in the crevices inside. Pick this out with your fingers, feeling around carefully to make sure that you do not include any splinters of shell with the meat.

8 Take the empty shell. On the underside you will notice that there is a distinct separation line running around the border. Tap the shell firmly with a wooden mallet or the end of your rolling pin so that it breaks off at this line. Alternatively, use a pair of flat-nosed pliers to snap the shell off level with the line, piece by piece. Scrub interior of shell thoroughly with a brush and make sure there is nothing left in the crevices. Scrub exterior of shell, using a light abrasive if necessary, to remove any dissolved patches. Dry shell thoroughly. Polish the outer surface with a wad of kitchen paper soaked in olive oil.

Dressed crab

The usual way of serving dressed crab in the shell is as follows:

1 Shell crab as directed above, keeping white and brown meat separate.

2 Trim and polish shell.

3 Mix white meat with a well-flavoured lemon mayonnaise (pp.36–7, Steps 5 to 7) in the proportion of 3 level tablespoons mayonnaise to 4oz meat. Correct seasoning if necessary with salt and pepper.

4 Dark meat should be dressed with a piquant sauce, e.g. Ravigote, in the proportion of 2 tablespoons to 4oz meat. Add a few drops more of wine vinegar and correct seasoning.

5 The dressed white meat is filled into either side of the crab shell, leaving a central panel clear for the dark meat.

6 Hard-boiled egg white chopped with a stainless steel knife is strewn thickly over the white sections, and sieved egg yolks are used to cover the dark panel in the centre.

7 As a final touch, sprinkle a thin line of finely chopped parsley down the two sides where white meat meets dark.

Délices de crabe

Basic crabmeat filling
One 7¾oz can crabmeat
Milk
1 bay leaf
½ chicken stock cube
Small strip of lemon zest
1–2 parsley sprigs
1 small onion, quartered
1oz butter
1oz flour
1 level teaspoon tomato concentrate
4–6 level tablespoons double cream
2 teaspoons brandy
Salt and freshly ground black pepper
Pinch of cayenne
Squeeze of lemon juice
Oil

We have no less than three ways of presenting this dish. In the first and simplest version, the creamy crabmeat filling is rolled into balls, egg-and-breadcrumbed and deep-fried. Or you can roll each portion up in a thin crêpe, coat with egg and breadcrumbs, and deep-fry again. The third variation turns the crab into a delicious, crisp, Middle Eastern *börek*. All three make excellent appetisers or 'fingerfood' to serve with drinks.

1 Drain juices from can of crabmeat into a measuring jug and make up to $\frac{1}{4}$ pint with milk. Pour into a pan. Add the next five ingredients; bring to the boil over a low heat. Remove; cover and leave to infuse for ten minutes.

2 Meanwhile, pick over crabmeat, removing any stray pieces of shell or cartilage.

3 In a medium-sized pan, melt butter. Blend in flour with a wooden spoon and cook over a low heat, stirring, for two to three minutes to make a pale *roux*.

4 Strain infused milk. Add to *roux* gradually, stirring vigorously to prevent lumps forming. Bring to the boil and cook, stirring constantly, for two to three minutes. Sauce will be very thick indeed. Remove from heat.

5 Beat in tomato concentrate, double cream and brandy, and when smooth, mix in crabmeat. Season to taste with salt if necessary, freshly ground black pepper and a pinch of cayenne, and sharpen flavour with a squeeze of lemon juice.

6 Grease a flat plate lightly with oil. Spread crabmeat mixture out on it evenly into a circle roughly 7in in diameter. Cool. Cover tightly with foil or plastic wrap and chill until firm.

Deep-fried crabmeat balls

Makes 24 balls
1 recipe *crabmeat filling* (p.124)
Beaten egg
Fine white breadcrumbs
Oil for deep-frying

1 Divide cold crabmeat mixture into twenty-four equal portions. Roll into balls.

2 Dip each ball in beaten egg; lift out with a slotted spoon and roll in breadcrumbs. Repeat egg-and-breadcrumbing once more.

3 Arrange crabmeat balls on a plate and chill while you heat oil for deep-frying.

4 Heat pan of oil to 375°F.

5 Deep-fry crabmeat balls, a portion at a time, for two or three minutes, or until crisp and golden. Drain on absorbent paper and serve immediately.

Crab börek

Makes 24 börek
1 recipe *crabmeat filling* (p.124)
12 sheets phyllo pastry (see Note)
About 6oz melted butter

Greek pastry known as 'phyllo' or 'filo' is an almost transparent, paper-like pastry, very similar to strudel dough in appearance. It can be bought from Cypriot shops in this country in tightly rolled, standard-size sheets sealed in cellophane. Any left over should be resealed carefully in plastic or foil as it becomes brittle and useless if left exposed to the air for any length of time. Always brush Greek pastry with a little melted butter before using it (to make pastry more pliable).

1 Preheat oven to fairly hot (425°F Mark 7).

2 Divide cold crabmeat mixture into twenty-four equal portions. Roll into balls.

3 Take one sheet of phyllo pastry at a time, keeping remainder wrapped in a damp cloth to prevent it drying out (see note above). Cut it in half lengthwise.

4 To shape *börek*: brush a half-sheet of phyllo with melted butter. Place a ball of crabmeat mixture in one corner, slightly off centre and 1in in from the edge. Fold sheet over it so that it is halved lengthwise again. You now have a long strip of pastry. Brush with

more melted butter. Take the short end with filling and fold it over slightly to seal in filling. Then take the (same) end and fold it over itself, making a triangle. Continue folding the strip over and over on to itself, keeping it in the shape of the triangle. Tuck in the end neatly.

5 Arrange triangles on a buttered baking sheet and brush tops all over with more melted butter.

6 Bake *börek* for ten to fifteen minutes until puffed and golden.

Note: If not to be served immediately, the unbaked pastries may be stored in the refrigerator so that they are cooked just before serving.

Mussels

It's a pity mussels are so cheap. Perhaps if they weren't, people would appeciate them more, for they are very fine indeed, especially in late autumn and during the winter.

People tend to be nervous about mussels, having heard that they can be dangerous if taken from polluted waters, but you have no grounds for worrying about those you buy in shops – by law these have to undergo thorough cleansing in special sea water tanks before they reach the public.

What you do have to be careful about is the odd dead mussel in a batch. This can be dangerous, as they go off quickly, so to be on the safe side, discard any that (*a*) are not tightly closed by the time you've finished scrubbing and 'bearding' them; and (*b*) any that are *still* closed at the end of cooking.

To clean mussels Equip yourself with a hard scrubbing brush. Put the mussels in the kitchen sink and scrub them one by one under running cold water. Be really conscientious about this, for any sand that remains on their shells is likely to find its way into the finished dish.

As you scrub each mussel, pull away the dark, frond-like 'beard' with the help of a short-bladed knife.

Drop each mussel into a large bowl of clear water as you prepare it.

To steam mussels open This is quite easy. Simply take a heavy-based saucepan with a tight-fitting lid. Add the mussels, together with flavouring herbs, wine, a little chopped shallot, or whatever your recipe calls for. Cover pan tightly.

Set pan over a high heat and cook the mussels, shaking the pan gently from time to time, for no more than five to seven minutes. By this time all the mussels that are going to open will have opened.

Discard any that are still tightly closed.

Don't overcook mussels or they will be tough and a lot of flavour will have been lost.

Moules farcies

Serves 2
24 large live mussels
Butter
1 shallot, finely chopped
4 tablespoons dry white wine
$\frac{1}{4}$ level teaspoon dried thyme
Small piece of bay leaf
2–4 level tablespoons finely chopped parsley
2 plump cloves garlic
2 teaspoons lemon juice
2oz stale white breadcrumbs
Salt and freshly ground black pepper

Mussels in bubbling hot garlic butter, with a crisp coating of golden brown breadcrumbs.

1 Scrub mussels clean under cold running water and remove 'beards'. Discard any that are not tightly closed by the end of this operation.

2 Melt $\frac{1}{2}$oz butter in a wide, heavy pan with a tight-fitting lid, and sauté finely chopped shallot until golden. Stir in dry white wine, thyme and bay leaf, and half the finely chopped parsley, and

simmer for one minute. Add mussels, cover tightly and cook over a high heat, shaking pan frequently, for five to seven minutes, or until mussels have all opened. Discard any that are still closed.

3 Drain mussels and carefully remove top shell from each one.

4 Peel and crush garlic cloves to a paste and add them to $\frac{1}{4}$lb butter, together with the remaining parsley, and beat until smooth and well blended.

5 Slip a piece of garlic butter over each mussel in its half-shell and arrange them side by side in a wide, heatproof dish. Sprinkle with lemon juice; scatter breadcrumbs over the top and season with salt and freshly ground black pepper.

6 Cook under a hot grill until butter has melted and breadcrumbs are sizzling and golden brown. Serve immediately.

Moules au safran

Serves 4
3–4 pints mussels
$\frac{1}{4}$ pint dry white wine
Bouquet garni (1 sprig parsley, 1 sprig thyme, 1 bay leaf)
2- 3 level tablespoons finely chopped parsley, to garnish

Sauce
1 Spanish onion, finely chopped
1 clove garlic, crushed
2 level tablespoons butter
Generous pinch of cayenne pepper
$\frac{1}{4}$ level teaspoon powdered saffron
$\frac{1}{4}$ pint double cream
1 egg yolk
Salt and freshly ground black pepper

Half the fun of this mussel dish, a cross between a soup and a stew similar to a *mouclade*, is using your fingers, so large napkins and finger bowls are a necessity. Serve with fresh French bread to mop up the delicious sauce.

1 Scrub mussels clean and remove 'beards'. Discard any shells that are cracked or that have not closed tightly by the end of this operation.

2 Put mussels in a heavy pan with a tight-fitting lid. Add half the wine and a bouquet garni; cover and cook over a high heat, shaking pan frequently, for five to seven minutes, or until mussels have all opened. Discard any that remain closed – they, too, are suspect.

3 Take mussels from the pan, shaking back any liquor left in their shells. Remove top shell from each mussel and arrange mussels in a wide serving dish. Keep hot. Strain liquor through a sieve lined with fine muslin.

4 To make sauce: in a heavy pan, simmer finely chopped onion and crushed garlic in butter until transparent.

5 Moisten with strained mussel liquor and remaining wine; add cayenne and saffron, and cook over a fairly high heat for five minutes until reduced by about one-third.

6 Stir in cream; bring to the boil again and remove from heat.

7 Beat in the egg yolk and season to taste with salt and freshly ground black pepper.

8 Pour sauce over mussels; sprinkle dish generously with finely chopped parsley and serve immediately.

Salade de moules

Serves 4
2 quarts mussels
2 level tablespoons finely chopped shallots
2 sprigs parsley
$\frac{1}{4}$ level teaspoon thyme
1 bay leaf
Salt and freshly ground black pepper
4–6 tablespoons dry white wine

2 tablespoons wine vinegar
Olive oil
2 level tablespoons coarsely chopped parsley

1 Scrub mussels thoroughly under cold running water and remove
'beards'. Discard any that are cracked or still open by the end of
this operation.

2 Place mussels in a large, heavy pan with a tight-fitting lid. Add
finely chopped shallots, parsley, thyme and bay leaf; season very
lightly with salt and freshly ground black pepper, and moisten
with dry white wine.

3 Cover pan tightly. Place over a high heat and cook for five to
seven minutes, or until mussels have opened. Discard any that
remain closed – they, too, are suspect.

4 Remove pan from heat. As soon as mussels can be handled, scoop
them out of their shells with a teaspoon into a bowl. You may, if
you wish, pull off their dark little outer frills, but this is not
necessary. Cover and keep warm.

5 Taste mussel liquor. If it is not too salty, boil it for a few minutes
to reduce it and intensify the flavour. Pour a little mussel liquor
through a sieve lined with double-thick muslin or a piece of
kitchen paper. If very salty, add a little more dry white wine.

6 Combine 2 tablespoons each mussel liquor and wine vinegar in
a small bowl. Beat in enough olive oil to make a good dressing.
Stir in half the chopped parsley and season to taste with salt and
freshly ground black pepper.

7 Pour dressing over warm mussels; toss lightly to coat them
evenly and allow to cool. Then chill until ready to serve.

8 Just before serving, arrange mussels in a shallow serving dish and
garnish with remaining parsley. Serve very cold.

Lobster

To choose a lobster

Live A live lobster should be vigorous and active. If its movements are weak and sluggish, this is an indication that it has been out of the water for some time and that it may already have been living off its own reserves (for which *you* are now being asked to pay) for weeks. So above all, make sure it's still heavy for its size.

Boiled Weight is again the only sure test of quality. To check for freshness, pull the tail out straight and let go: it should spring back sharply into its original position, i.e. pressed tightly against the body.

To boil a lobster

Plunge the lobster (live) into a large pan of boiling salted water to which you have added a few peppercorns, a bay leaf and a sprig of thyme. Bring back to the boil again quickly, and poach for five minutes per lb. *Don't* overcook.

To shell a boiled lobster

Equip yourself with a cleaver (or, failing this, a heavy knife with a strong blade), a teaspoon, a metal skewer or a wooden toothpick or two, a rolling pin, a wooden board on which to work, a small bowl and a plate.

1 Lay lobster on the board, with its hump facing upwards, and with the cleaver split it in half lengthwise, severing the shell and meat at the same time.

2 Take one lobster-half at a time. With your finger, scoop out the stomach, which is to be found almost immediately behind the head and looks just like a little greaseproof paper bag. Somewhere in the vicinity, you should be able to locate the intestinal vein. Remove this as well.

3 With your teaspoon, scrape out the creamy, grey-green matter in the chest and put it in the bowl. Add to this any bright red coral (this is the roe, so it will only be present in a female lobster).

4 Break off the pliable tail from the chest. Scoop out meat from half-tails, using either the skewer or the teaspoon, and keeping pieces as large as possible. Place meat on the plate and discard any small pieces of shell.

5 Break off the claws together with the hinged double-joints that connect them to the chest. Separate claws from double-joints.

6 Split joints in two. Remove meat with skewer and add to the plate.

7 Now take a claw. Gently prise the smaller part back on itself to separate it from the main claw. As it comes away, it will draw a large, fan-like piece of cartilage out of the main part of the claw. Discard this and skewer flesh out of the smaller claw. Add to plate.

8 Crack the larger claw with a whack or two of your cleaver or rolling pin. Prise off shell, keeping pieces of meat as large as possible. Add to plate.

9 Now take pieces of chest. Pull off the outer shell. If there is any more creamy substance adhering to the outer shell, scrape this off and add to the bowl containing coral.

10 Pull off the four spidery legs attached to each side of the chest.

11 With your skewer or toothpick, scrape meat out of chest, digging into the crevices of the rib-like cartilage with your skewer to extract every morsel. Add meat to plate.

12 Finally, take each leg and divide it into joints. Lay joints, one at a time, on your board and, with the rolling pin, roll over them firmly in one direction so that meat is squeezed out. Add to plate.

A cooked lobster weighing about 12oz in the shell will provide you with about 6oz meat.

Simple boiled lobster – hot

Serves 4
2 live lobsters (about 2lb each)
Boiling salted water, or a well-flavoured *court-bouillon*
  (p.135)
Melted butter
Lemon juice
Salt, paprika and cayenne pepper
Finely chopped fresh tarragon or chives

One of the most delicious shellfish dishes in the world. But very expensive. You can procure live lobsters from your fishmonger, but they have to be ordered well in advance.

1 Fill a large saucepan three-quarters full of salted water, or a well-flavoured *court-bouillon* and bring to the boil. (Along the southern coast of France, they sometimes cook live lobsters in a highly flavoured *soupe de poissons* mixture complete with *rouille*. It makes a wonderfully aromatic dish.)

2 Plunge the lobsters, head first, into the boiling liquid; bring to the boil again and boil quickly for one minute; then lower heat and simmer gently for twenty-five minutes, removing any scum that rises during cooking.

3 Remove cooked lobsters; drain well and rub shell with a little melted butter to make it shine.

4 Crack claws and split body in half down the middle, removing intestine, stomach and the spongy looking gills (as directed on p.132).

5 Place the prepared lobster halves on a heated serving dish; brush meat with a little melted butter and serve immediately with a piquant sauce made of additional melted butter, flavoured with lemon juice and salt, paprika and cayenne pepper, to taste. When available, add a little finely chopped fresh tarragon or chives.

Wine court-bouillon for fish

1 bottle dry white wine
$\frac{3}{4}$ pint water
$\frac{1}{4}$lb carrots, sliced
$\frac{1}{4}$lb onions, sliced
1 handful parsley stalks
1 bay leaf
1 sprig thyme
Coarse salt
12 fennel seeds (optional)
12 peppercorns
Pinch of cayenne pepper

1 Combine ingredients in a large saucepan or fish kettle and bring to the boil. Skim, and boil for forty-five minutes.

2 Strain and cool.

Note: For a simpler *court-bouillon* substitute water for dry white wine and add a little wine, wine vinegar or lemon juice, to taste.

Cold lobster mayonnaise

Serves 4
2 live lobsters (about 2lb each), cooked in boiling salted water
   or a well-flavoured *court-bouillon* as above
Olive oil
Lettuce leaves
Tomato wedges
Lemon wedges
1 recipe *mayonnaise* (see p.136)

Steps 1–3 in *simple boiled lobster* recipe (see p.136), rubbing cooked lobster shell with a little olive oil (instead of melted butter) to make it shine.

4 Place the prepared lobster halves on a serving dish; garnish dish with lettuce leaves and tomato and lemon wedges and serve with homemade mayonnaise.

Classic mayonnaise

Makes ½ pint
2 egg yolks
½ level teaspoon English or French mustard
Salt and freshly ground black pepper
Lemon juice
½ pint olive oil

1 Make sure all ingredients are at room temperature before you
  start.

2 Remove any gelatinous threads left on the egg yolks. Put yolks
  in a medium-sized bowl and set it on a damp cloth on the table to
  hold it steady. Add mustard and a pinch each of salt and freshly
  ground black pepper, and work to a smooth paste with a spoon or
  a wire whisk.

3 Add a teaspoon of lemon juice and work until smooth again.

4 Pour olive oil into a measuring jug. With a teaspoon, start adding
  oil to egg yolk mixture a drop at a time, beating well between each
  addition.

5 Having incorporated about a quarter of the oil, step up the rate at
  which you add the remainder of the oil, to a steady, fine trickle,
  beating strongly as you do so. If the mayonnaise should become
  very thick before all the oil has been absorbed, thin it down again
  with more lemon juice or a few drops of cold water. Forcing olive
  oil into a very thick mayonnaise is another factor which may cause
  it to curdle. The finished mayonnaise should be thick and shiny,
  and drop from the spoon or whisk in heavy globs.

6 Correct seasoning, adding more salt, freshly ground black pepper
  or lemon juice if necessary.

Lobster – New York style

Serves 4
2 cooked lobsters (about 2lb each)

4 level tablespoons butter
Juice of $\frac{1}{2}$ lemon
Paprika and cayenne pepper
4 tablespoons heated cognac
2 egg yolks, well beaten
$\frac{1}{2}$ pint double cream
Salt and freshly ground black pepper
Boiled rice
Lemon wedges

1 Cut cooked lobsters in half lengthwise. Crack claws. Remove lobster meat from the shells and cut into dice.

2 Melt butter and lemon juice in a frying-pan; add diced lobster meat and sauté for a few minutes. Flavour with a pinch each of Paprika and cayenne pepper. Flame with cognac. Keep warm.

3 Combine beaten egg yolks and double cream in the top of a double saucepan and cook over water, stirring constantly, until the mixture coats the back of a spoon. Do not let mixture come to the boil, or the sauce will curdle.

4 Add lobster meat and pan juices and heat through. Season to taste with salt, freshly ground black pepper, paprika and cayenne. Serve on a bed of boiled rice. Garnish dish with lemon wedges.

Seafood casserole

Serves 6
4 shallots, finely chopped
4 tablespoons butter
$\frac{1}{4}$ pint dry white wine
$\frac{1}{2}$lb button mushrooms, thinly sliced
1 pint thick Béchamel sauce (see p.138)
$\frac{1}{2}$lb cooked lobster, sliced
$\frac{1}{2}$lb shelled prawns
$\frac{1}{2}$lb cooked sole, sliced
$\frac{1}{2}$lb cooked scallops, sliced or quartered
24 mussels, cooked and shelled
Salt and freshly ground black pepper

1 In a saucepan, sauté shallots in half the butter until transparent; add wine and simmer until reduced to 2 or 3 tablespoons.

2 Sauté mushrooms in remaining butter until soft; add to shallot mixture.

3 Strain Béchamel sauce in a pan; carefully fold in prepared seafood, together with mushroom-shallot mixture.

4 Heat through gently, adding salt and freshly ground black pepper, to taste, and thinning sauce down with a little more dry white wine (or stock left over from cooking seafood) if mixture seems too thick.

5 Serve immediately with saffron rice and green peas.

Classic Béchamel sauce

Makes about 1 pint
Butter
½ Spanish onion, finely chopped
3 level tablespoons flour
1½ pints milk
2oz lean veal or ham, finely chopped
1 stalk celery, finely chopped
1 small sprig thyme
½ bay leaf
White peppercorns
Freshly grated nutmeg
Salt

Do not be tempted to shortcut the process of making this sauce – the slow reduction of fine sauces as exemplified in this recipe is one of the cardinal rules of great cooking.

1 In a thick-bottomed saucepan or in the top of a double saucepan, melt 3 level tablespoons butter over direct heat and sauté onion very gently until transparent but not coloured.

2 Add flour and continue to cook, stirring constantly, for a few minutes, taking great care not to let *roux* colour.

3 Scald milk and add to *roux* gradually, stirring constantly to prevent lumps forming. Continue to cook, stirring, until sauce becomes thick and smooth.

4 In another pan, simmer chopped lean veal (or ham) and celery in 1 level tablespoon butter over a very low heat. Add thyme, bay leaf, a few white peppercorns and a pinch of freshly grated nutmeg. Cook for five minutes, stirring to prevent veal from browning.

5 Combine contents of pan with sauce; mix well and bring to the boil over direct heat. Then cook over hot water for about one and a quarter hours, or until sauce is reduced to just over 1 pint. Season to taste with salt.

6 Strain sauce through a fine sieve into a bowl, pressing meat and onion with a wooden spoon to extract all their juices. If not using sauce immediately, cover surface with tiny pieces of butter to stop a skin from forming.

Great boiled dishes

The title of this lesson is something of a misnomer, for 'boiling' as such plays little or no part in the dishes that follow. In some cases one does boil, but only for a carefully limited time, in order to force out scum.

The crucial lesson to be learned here, as in so many branches of cooking, is control of heat. Once you have done with any initial fast boiling, the liquid in your pot should *never* again be allowed to progress beyond a light shudder, with tiny bubbles breaking here and there on the surface at irregular intervals. If you can't get the heat of your stove low enough to achieve this (and if you're cooking on gas, do make sure there are no draughts to puff out the tiny flame), try using an asbestos mat or, if that doesn't help, raise the pot slightly above the cooking top by standing it on a trivet or metal rack.

Meat subjected to this almost imperceptible cooking remains tender and juicy instead of being reduced to a bundle of tough, dry rag – as inevitably happens if it is allowed to boil fast.

Skimming

The important points to remember when skimming stock are:

1 To use salt – with discretion – to force out scum without oversalting the stock itself. (Bear in mind that the stock will probably reduce quite considerably during cooking so that what tastes adequately salted at the beginning will be oversalty by the end.)

2 To refrain from skimming until foam on the surface becomes a definite scum that won't slip through the holes in your slotted spoon.

Preparing the meats

If you are using different meats in pieces of vastly varying size, it is a good idea to divide the larger ones so that all the lumps are roughly the same size, say 2lb in weight. This gives you a better chance of having everything in the pot ready at the same time.

To make it easier to test the various meats for doneness, tie a string around each piece, leaving one end long enough to hang over the side of the pot so that you can draw out any piece you wish to test without trouble.

* The 'boiled' dishes we have given below may at first glance appear quite a to-do. But don't forget that in many of them, you are getting a *whole* main course, vegetables and all, from one pot, plus a bonus of rich stock to serve as a soup on its own, or to use for cooking and flavouring a pot of rice, or to turn into a sauce, or to keep for later use as the foundation of some other delicious soup.

Boiled collar of bacon with horseradish cream sauce

Serves 4–6
One 2lb piece collar of bacon
1 onion, quartered
1 bay leaf
2 cloves
2 blades mace

Horseradish cream sauce
1 pint milk
1 chicken stock cube
1 small onion, finely chopped
3 level tablespoons butter
4 level tablespoons flour

¼ pint single cream
Grated horseradish
Wine vinegar or lemon juice
Salt and freshly ground black pepper

1 Soak collar of bacon overnight in a large bowl of water, changing it as often as possible.

2 The following day, drain bacon thoroughly and place it in a pan with cold water to cover. Bring slowly to the boil; drain again and cover with fresh water. Add quartered onion, bay leaf, cloves and mace; bring gently to the boil again and simmer very slowly, allowing twenty minutes per pound, plus twenty minutes over – i.e. one hour for a 2lb joint.

3 About half an hour before the end of cooking time, prepare sauce: combine milk and stock cube in a pan, and bring to the boil, stirring until cube has dissolved.

4 In another, medium-sized pan, simmer finely chopped onion in butter over a very low heat for ten minutes, or until soft and transparent but not coloured.

5 Blend in flour and continue to stir over a low heat for two to three minutes to make a pale *roux*.

6 Gradually add hot, flavoured milk, stirring vigorously to prevent flour forming lumps, and when sauce is smooth, blend in cream.

7 Add horseradish to taste. The amount will depend on the type of horseradish you have been able to get – freshly grated, packed in vinegar, or dehydrated. Simmer gently for ten minutes, stirring occasionally.

8 Flavour sauce with white wine vinegar or lemon juice, again depending on how your horseradish was prepared. Season lightly with salt and freshly ground black pepper.

9 When bacon joint is tender, remove strings; pull off rind – it will come away easily if joint is sufficiently cooked.

10 Place bacon joint on a heated serving dish and serve hot, with the sauce handed round separately.

Boiled forehock of bacon with fruit sauce

Serves 4
1 smoked bacon forehock, about 1¾lb (see note)
1 medium-sized onion, quartered
4 black peppercorns
2 cloves
1 bay leaf

Fruit sauce
One 12oz can pineapple cubes
1 orange
1 level tablespoon cornflour
1 level tablespoon Demerara sugar
1 tablespoon soy sauce
2 tablespoons olive oil
1–2 tablespoons white wine vinegar
Salt and freshly ground black pepper

For this dish, you can use a 'boil-in-the-bag' joint.

1 Pierce bag containing bacon joint; place it in a pan with water to cover; add quartered onion, peppercorns, cloves and bay leaf. Bring to the boil slowly; turn down heat and simmer gently for about thirty minutes per pound, or until cooked through but not stringy.

2 To make fruit sauce: drain can of pineapple cubes, reserving syrup in a measuring jug. Cut each pineapple cube in four.

3 Finely grate rind from orange on to a plate. Peel orange and divide into segments, holding it over the measuring jug as you do so to catch any juice that may escape. Cut each orange segment in half.

4 Make syrup and orange juice up to ¼ pint with water if necessary.

5 In a small pan, blend remaining sauce ingredients together smoothly. Gradually add pineapple syrup mixture and bring to the boil, stirring constantly. Simmer, stirring, for two to three minutes.

6 Gently stir in pineapple and orange segments. If necessary, thin sauce with a tablespoon or two of the bacon stock. Flavour to taste with a pinch of grated orange rind and season with salt and freshly ground black pepper.

7 When bacon is tender, drain bag and remove it. Pull skin off joint – it will strip away easily if bacon is sufficiently cooked.

8 Place joint on a heated serving dish and serve immediately, accompanied by sauce in a separate heated sauceboat or bowl.

Boiled knuckle of bacon with parsley sauce

Serves 3–4
1 smoked 'boil-in-the-bag' bacon knuckle, 2–2¼lb
1 medium-sized onion, quartered
4 black peppercorns
2 cloves
1 bay leaf

Parsley sauce
3 level tablespoons butter
2 level tablespoons flour
½ pint milk
3–4 level tablespoons finely chopped parsley
Salt and freshly ground black pepper

1 Boil the bacon knuckle in its bag (pierced) as directed in the recipe for *boiled forehock of bacon* (see p.143), allowing thirty minutes per pound.

2 About fifteen minutes before bacon is due to finish cooking, prepare parsley sauce: in a heavy pan, melt butter, blend in flour and cook over a low heat, stirring constantly, for two to three minutes to make a pale *roux*.

3 Gradually add milk, stirring vigorously to prevent lumps forming. Bring to the boil, stirring; add finely chopped parsley and continue to simmer, stirring frequently, for three to four minutes until sauce is thick and smooth, and no longer tastes floury. Season lightly with salt and freshly ground black pepper.

4 Serve bacon as above, accompanied by sauce in a separate, heated sauceboat.

Boiled fresh ox tongue

Serves 6–8
1 fresh ox tongue, 4–4½lb
1 Spanish onion, quartered
2 leeks, trimmed
2 carrots, cut into chunks
2 stalks celery, cut into chunks
3 level tablespoons coarse sea salt (gros sel)

Bouquet garni
About 8 sprigs parsley
1 level teaspoon dried thyme
2 bay leaves
1 (unpeeled) clove garlic
6 allspice berries
6 black peppercorns

1 Scrub tongue with a stiff brush under cold running water to clean it thoroughly, and trim away any gristle or excess fat from root or underside. Then leave tongue to soak in a bowl of cold water for one hour.

2 Meanwhile, prepare vegetables and tie the components of your bouquet garni up in a piece of muslin.

3 Drain tongue and fit it into a large cooking pot with 8 pints cold water. Add coarse sea salt and bring to the boil over a low heat, skimming frequently as liquid approaches boiling point until surface is clear of froth.

4 As soon as liquid starts simmering, add vegetables and bouquet garni. Keep liquid at a gentle simmer for the next three and a half to four hours.

5 To test if tongue is cooked, pull at the little bones embedded at the the root. They should come out easily and cleanly.

6 When tongue is cooked, lift it out of the pot, allowing all the stock to drain back – this can be used to make an accompanying sauce, or kept for soup. Rinse tongue briefly under the cold tap so that surface is cool enough to handle. Peel skin off in strips. It should come away very easily, but it may be necessary here and there to pare it off with a knife. Tongue is now ready to serve.

Pickled ox tongue

Serves 6–8
1 fresh ox tongue, 4–4½lb
Coarse sea salt (gros sel)

Pickling brine
6oz coarse sea salt
3oz Demerara sugar
½oz saltpetre (potassium nitrate)
1 bay leaf
6 black peppercorns
3 juniper berries

1 The day before immersing the tongue in brine, scrub it thoroughly under cold running water. Trim root and underside. Pat tongue dry. Prick all over with a skewer and rub liberally with coarse salt. Place tongue in a bowl; cover and leave overnight in a cool place.

2 The following day, prepare pickling brine: combine ingredients in a pan with 4 pints cold water. Bring to the boil over a low heat; boil for two to three minutes; remove from heat and leave until quite cold.

3 Rinse tongue thoroughly. Place it in a large glazed bowl. Strain cold brine over it and, if neceessary, weight tongue so that it is

completely submerged. Cover bowl tightly with plastic wrap or foil. Leave in a cool place for seven days.

Before proceeding to cook pickled tongue, rinse it thoroughly under the cold tap and leave to soak for one hour in a bowl of cold water.

Note: You can obtain saltpetre from any well-stocked chemist.

Boiled pickled tongue

A pickled tongue is boiled in exactly the same way as a fresh one (see p.145), except that for obvious reasons the salt is omitted from the stock.

Boiled ox tongue and carrots with horseradish chantilly

Boil a fresh or pickled tongue as directed in the master recipe (p.145).

About thirty minutes before tongue is cooked, scrape 2–2½lb carrots; cut them in halves or quarters, according to size; place them in a pan and strain over enough of the tongue stock to cover. Boil carrots until tender. Drain.

Serve tongue on a large, heated platter surrounded by carrots, and accompanied by a bowl of *horseradish chantilly* (p.166).

Pressed tongue

Serves 6
1 pickled ox tongue, 4–4½lb, boiled (p.146)
1 packet aspic jelly powder, or enough to set ½ pint
2 tablespoons port or Madeira (optional)

As soon as tongue is cooked, lift out of the stock; skin it and remove any bones at the root. Trim root end neatly.

2 Select a deepish, round dish into which the tongue will just fit
   when curled up tightly. (For the size of tongue specified here use
   a soufflé dish 5½in in diameter.)

3 Curl hot tongue tightly into dish.

4 Bring cooking stock to the boil and cook rapidly, uncovered, to
   reduce it until either saltiness prevents you going further, or the
   stock juices taste rich and meaty.

5 Strain ½ pint reduced stock into a measuring jug. Add 1 packet
   aspic jelly powder, or enough to set ½ pint, and stir until dissolved.
   If liked, jelly may be flavoured with a little port or Madeira:
   remember when adding it – and any further seasonings – that the
   aspic will lose a lot of flavour once it sets.

6 Pour enough liquid aspic over tongue almost to cover it. Place a
   flat plate on top and weight down with cans until tongue is
   completely submerged. (Left-over aspic may be set on a plate; then
   chopped and used to decorate tongue.)

7 Cool tongue and chill until set.

8 To serve: dip mould for a few seconds in hot water and turn out
   on to a flat plate. Serve cut in thin slices, accompanied by pickles
   and salad.

Tongue with Italian green sauce

Serves 6–8
1 pickled tongue, 4–4½lb, boiled (p.146)

Italian green sauce
2 large bunches watercress
6 level tablespoons finely chopped parsley
1 level tablespoon grated onion
½ clove garlic, crushed
1 tablespoon lemon juice
12 tablespoons olive oil
8 anchovy fillets

1 level tablespoon roughly chopped capers
Salt and freshly ground black pepper

1 Prepare tongue as directed on pp.146–7.

2 Prepare Italian green sauce: rinse watercress in a colander under
cold running water until you are sure it is quite free of grit. Shake
dry and strip leaves from stalks.

3 Bring a pan of water to the boil. Throw in watercress leaves;
blanch for 1 minute; drain thoroughly in the colander and
'refresh' with cold water.

4 Combine blanched watercress, chopped parsley, onion, garlic and
lemon juice in the container of an electric blender. Set blender in
motion and, when contents are reduced to a purée pour in olive
oil slowly, a tablespoon at a time. Finally, add anchovy fillets
and blend until smooth.

5 Scrape sauce into a bowl. Stir in roughly chopped capers and
season with salt if necessary (anchovies may already have made
sauce salty enough) and freshly ground black pepper. You may
also prefer a little more lemon juice.

6 To serve: slice cold boiled pickled tongue and arrange in an
overlapping row on a serving dish. Spoon some of the sauce down
centre and serve remainder in a separate bowl or sauceboat.

Note: If you have no blender, sauce may either be pounded in a
mortar, or you can chop blanched watercress leaves as finely as
possible with the chopped parsley; then put them in a bowl and
whisk in remaining ingredients with a hand-held electric mixer, or
a rotary whisk.

Boiled lamb with dill sauce

Serves 6
1 leg of lamb, 3½–4lb
Salt and freshly ground black pepper
Bouquet garni (2 sprigs parsley, 2 stalks celery, 2 bay leaves,

coarsely chopped, 1 sprig thyme or ¼ level teaspoon dried
thyme)
2 Spanish onions, each stuck with a clove
Butter
1lb small carrots, scraped
1lb small onions, peeled
Finely chopped parsley, to garnish

Dill sauce
About 1 pint reduced lamb stock (see Step 10)
3 level tablespoons butter
3 level tablespoons flour
1–1½ teaspoons dried dill weed
2 egg yolks
¼ pint single cream
Salt and freshly ground black pepper
Squeeze of lemon juice

Mutton is, of course, *the* meat traditionally used for this great
Scandinavian dish, but as it is so difficult to get, we have used lamb,
which is even more succulent and no more expensive than mutton
nowadays.

1 Ask your butcher to remove shank bone from leg of lamb.

2 Trim most of fat from leg and shave away any official 'stamps'.
  Rub leg with salt and freshly ground black pepper. Wrap it up
  tightly in muslin and tie ends securely with string.

3 Tie components of bouquet garni in a twist of muslin.

4 Select a deep pan that will hold leg comfortably. Fill with water
  (allowing for displacement by the joint); salt it and bring to the boil.

5 Lower in the leg of lamb; bring back to the boil and boil
  vigorously for ten minutes, skimming off any scum that rises to
  the surface.

6 Reduce heat under pan to a bare simmer. Add bouquet garni and
  the onions stuck with cloves, and simmer very, very gently until

lamb is tender. There should be a suspicion of pink about the juices that run when you pierce it through to the centre with a skewer. Allow twenty-five to thirty minutes per pound.

7 About thirty minutes before lamb is due to finish cooking, pour 6 tablespoons of its stock into each of two medium-sized saucepans. Add 1 level tablespoon butter to each pan and melt over a high heat.

8 Place carrots in one pan and onions in the other. Lower heat to a gentle simmer. Push a sheet of buttered greaseproof paper down over contents of each pan; half-cover with a lid and cook gently, shaking pans frequently, for about twenty minutes until vegetables are just tender and all the stock has either evaporated or been absorbed. Vegetables should be *very* lightly glazed, if at all.

9 When leg of lamb is cooked, unwrap it and place it on a large, heated serving dish. Surround with cooked carrots and onions. Cover dish tightly with foil to prevent meat drying out and keep hot in a cool oven while you prepare the dill sauce.

10 Skin lamb stock of fat if necessary. Ladle 1½ pints of it through a sieve into a pan. Boil briskly until reduced by about one-third. Remove from heat.

11 To make dill sauce: in the top of a double saucepan, melt butter over direct heat. Blend in flour with a wooden spoon and stir over a low heat for two to three minutes to make a pale *roux*.

12 Gradually add reduced stock, stirring vigorously to prevent lumps forming, and bring to the boil, stirring until sauce is smooth and thickened.

13 Stir in dill – if you have not cooked with dill before, start with the smaller amount, then add more to taste if you wish – and simmer gently for two to three minutes.

14 Meanwhile, beat egg yolks and cream together until well mixed.

15 Remove pan from heat. Blend in egg and cream mixture; fit pan over simmering water and continue to cook gently for a further

four to five minutes until sauce has thickened again. Do not allow sauce to boil, or egg yolks may curdle. It should have a pleasant, thickish-coating consistency. If it is too thick, add a little more strained lamb stock.

16 Season sauce to taste with salt and freshly ground black pepper, and sharpen flavour with a squeeze of lemon juice. Pour into a heated sauce boat.

17 To serve: garnish lamb and vegetables with finely chopped parsley and serve accompanied by dill sauce.

Boiled chicken with lemon cream sauce

Serves 4–6
One 5–5½lb boiling fowl, dressed weight
1 Spanish onion, stuck with 2 cloves
2 large carrots, scraped or peeled
1 stalk celery, cut into 2in lengths
2 cloves garlic, peeled
2 pints chicken (cube) stock
¼ pint dry white wine
4–6 black peppercorns
Butter

Lemon cream sauce
3 level tablespoons butter
3 level tablespoons flour
¾ pint stock (from casserole), strained
1 tablespoon lemon juice
Salt and freshly ground black pepper
2 egg yolks

Serve the chicken on a bed of saffron rice or, more adventurously, with rice flavoured with pine nuts and a handful of currants. Recipes below.

1 Clean and truss boiling fowl if necessary.

2 In a casserole just large enough to hold the fowl comfortably,

combine onion, carrots, celery, garlic, chicken stock, dry white wine and peppercorns, and bring to the boil.

3 Place fowl on its side in the liquor. Bring back to the boil and immediately turn down heat so that fowl barely simmers.

4 Cover exposed side of bird with a sheet of buttered greaseproof paper. Put on the lid and simmer for two and a half hours, turning chicken over on to its other side at the half-way stage.

5 About ten minutes before cooking time of fowl is up, start the rice (see p.154), pouring off $\frac{3}{4}$ pint simmering stock from the casserole as you need it, and leaving fowl to carry on barely simmering over a low heat.

6 While rice is cooking, prepare lemon cream sauce: in a heavy-based pan, melt butter; blend in flour with a wooden spoon and stir over a low heat for two to three minutes to make a pale *roux*. Remove from heat.

7 Pour off a further $\frac{3}{4}$ pint stock from casserole. (Again, let the fowl continue to cook – or rather keep hot – in the remains of the simmering stock.)

8 Return *roux* to a low heat. Gradually strain in stock, stirring vigorously to prevent lumps forming. Bring to the boil and simmer gently, stirring, for three to four minutes. Add lemon juice; season to taste with salt and freshly ground black pepper, and remove from heat.

9 Whisk egg yolks in a small bowl. Whisk in a little of the hot sauce; then blend with remaining sauce in the pan (still *off* the heat). Keep hot over hot water while you dish up bird and rice.

10 To serve: drain fowl thoroughly of remaining stock and arrange it on a large, heated serving dish. Mix 1 to 2 level tablespoons butter into rice with a fork, and spoon around bird.

11 Mask bird with some of the sauce and serve immediately, accompanied by remaining sauce in a heated sauceboat.

Saffron rice

¾ pint stock (from casserole), strained
Generous pinch of saffron strands
1 level tablespoon butter
1 Spanish onion, finely chopped
8oz long-grain rice
Salt and freshly ground black pepper
Freshly grated nutmeg

1 Pour a little of the hot, strained stock over saffron strands in a cup and leave to 'infuse' until required.

2 Melt butter in a heavy, medium-sized pan with a tight-fitting lid, and simmer finely chopped onion until transparent but not coloured, two to three minutes.

3 Add rice and stir over a low heat until grains are coated with buttery juice. Remove from heat.

4 Mash saffron strands against sides of cup with a spoon to extract as much colour as possible.

5 Add saffron mixture to rice, together with remaining hot stock. Season to taste with salt, freshly ground black pepper and a pinch of freshly grated nutmeg. Bring to the boil and reduce heat to a slow simmer.

6 Cover pan tightly and leave rice to simmer undisturbed for fifteen to twenty minutes, or until liquid has been absorbed, leaving rice tender but not mushy.

Pilaff with pine nuts and currants

1 level tablespoon butter
1 tablespoon olive oil
2oz pine nuts
8oz long-grain rice
1oz currants
¾ pint boiling stock (from casserole), strained
Salt and freshly ground black pepper

1 Heat butter and oil together in a heavy, medium-sized pan with a tight-fitting lid. Add pine nuts and sauté gently until golden but not brown.

2 Add rice and currants, and stir over a moderate heat for two to three minutes longer until grains are transparent and thoroughly coated with hot fat.

3 Add boiling stock. Season to taste with salt and freshly ground black pepper; bring back to the boil; reduce heat to a bare simmer and cover tightly with the lid.

4 Leave rice to simmer undisturbed for fifteen to twenty minutes, or until stock has been absorbed, leaving rice tender but not mushy.

Pot-au-feu

Serves 4–6
2lb beef for pot-au-feu (see note)
1lb shin of beef on the bone
1lb shin of veal on the bone
2oz ox liver
1 chicken liver
3 large carrots
1 large or 2 small turnips
2 large leeks
2 stalks celery
Coarse salt
2–3 sprigs parsley
1 sprig thyme or a pinch of dried thyme
1 small bay leaf
1 Spanish onion, stuck with 1 clove
1 fat clove garlic

To serve
Coarse salt and freshly ground black pepper
Various mustards and pickles
Horseradish chantilly (p.166)

A pot-au-feu may seem quite a performance at first sight, but remember that you are getting two dishes for the price of one: a rich bouillon to start with, followed by a steaming platter of beef and vegetables.

The English cuts of beef most closely resembling the *tranche grasse*, *gîte à la noix* and *paleron* or *macreuse* traditionally used by French cooks for a *pot-au-feu* are, respectively, thick flank, silverside and blade bone or chuck, but you can also use brisket, top rib, top round or shoulder, or a combination of two of these when preparing a double portion of the recipe, plus shin of beef and shin of veal with their bones for the gelatinous content.

1 Ask your butcher to roll and tie each piece of meat so that it holds its shape during cooking. The pieces of shin should first be boned and the bones chopped into large chunks. When making *pot-au-feu* for a larger number of people, the beef should be divided up so that no piece weighs more than about 2lb; otherwise it will be difficult to calculate the cooking time. It is also a good idea to leave a length of string attached to each piece of beef to allow you to fish it out of the pot when you want to test it.

2 Put the bones in a large pot (for the ingredients listed, I used a two-gallon pot), and lay the meat and livers on top. Add 5 pints cold water, or a combination of water and light stock if you have some handy. Bring to a simmer over a *very* low heat.

3 Meanwhile, peel carrots and turnip(s), and quarter them lengthwise. Split leeks down the centre and wash them thoroughly under cold running water. Trim and wash celery stalks.

4 Reassemble leeks, sandwiching a celery stalk inside each one, and tie them together firmly with string. If the bundle won't fit your pot whole, cut it in half.

5 When the water begins to shudder, add a little salt to help the scum disengage itself from the meat and bones – not too much, though, for the liquid will reduce during cooking and may end up too salty. At first, a white foam will rise to the surface. Curb your impatience until this forms itself into a distinct scum, otherwise it will slip through your slotted spoon when you try to skim it off. On the other hand, don't wait too long before skimming, or the

scum will disperse throughout the liquid again and make your stock cloudy. Skim several times, each time adding $\frac{1}{4}$ pint cold water to settle the surface for a few moments and bring a new rise of scum to the surface, until only a little white froth remains. Don't worry about this; it will of its own accord be consumed in the cooking. Finally, wipe the sides of the pot clean.

6 Add carrots and turnips, parsley, thyme and a small bay leaf; bring back to the boil very slowly and skim again if necessary. Then put the lid on at a tilt to allow steam to escape and leave for one hour, occasionally checking that the pot has not started boiling.

7 After the first hour, add leek bundles, the onion stuck with a clove and garlic. Leave the pot to tremble gently as before for a further two hours, or until meat and vegetables are tender.

8 When ready to serve: lift meat and vegetables out of the pot, letting them drain back into it. Discard strings; cut each piece of meat into serving pieces and arrange in the centre of a large, hot platter. Surround meat with the vegetables, grouping them by colour. Moisten with a little of the stock; cover the platter with foil and keep hot.

9 Remove grease from stock; strain stock through a muslin-lined sieve and reheat it.

10 Serve the stock first, followed by the platter of beef and vegetables, accompanied by coarse salt, a large peppermill, various mustards and pickles, and my own favourite accompaniment for *pot-au-feu*, *horseradish chantilly*.

Note: Cabbage, not usually a part of a classic *pot-au-feu* but excellent with it nevertheless, should be cooked separately, as its flavour would overpower the stock. Cook wedges in water first; then finish them in a little of the stock poured off into another pan, and serve with meat and vegetables. The platter can also be garnished with some boiled or steamed potatoes.

Boeuf bouilli
(Boiled beef)

Serves 4
2lb beef, topside, flank or brisket
Bouquet garni (parsley, thyme, bay leaf)
1 onion, stuck with 2 cloves
1 stalk celery, halved
3 large carrots, halved
2 large turnips, halved or quartered
4 leeks, trimmed and cut in three
½lb shin of beef
Salt and freshly ground black pepper
2 large marrow bones
6 small slices bread, trimmed of crusts

1 Put the topside, flank or brisket of beef, the bouquet garni and the onion stuck with cloves in a large pan or stock pot. Add 4 pints water and bring to the boil over a very low heat, allowing the scum to accumulate on the surface. When a thick skin has formed, pour in about ¼ pint cold water to stop the stock from boiling any further, and skim scum off carefully with a slotted spoon.

2 Bring to the boil again, still keeping heat under pan very low, and add the prepared vegetables and the shin of beef. Simmer very slowly for three hours – the more gentle the heat, the clearer your stock will be.

3 After two hours' simmering, add salt and freshly ground black pepper to taste.

4 Twenty minutes before the end of cooking time, tie the marrow bones in a piece of muslin to prevent marrow seeping out into the stock. Add them to the pot and simmer for twenty minutes.

5 Meanwhile, toast bread slices. Heat a shallow serving dish.

6 Remove marrow bones from the pan, unwrap muslin and scoop out marrow. Spread it on toast and cut in half to make triangles. Sprinkle lightly with salt.

Arrange meat and vegetables on the serving dish, and garnish with toast triangles. Serve very hot, preceded by cups of hot stock, which you have first skimmed of excess fat.

Boeuf à la ficelle

Serves 4

1lb carrots
1lb small, sweet turnips
2 pints well-flavoured beef stock (p.160)
8oz small white button mushrooms
4 tournedos steaks, about 6oz each
4 thin strips pork fat
Freshly ground black pepper
4 teaspoons brandy

Boeuf à la ficelle or 'beef on a string' takes its name from the length of string on which the steak is suspended as it poaches gently in a well-flavoured beef stock.

Peel carrots. Cut them into $\frac{1}{4}$in thick slices, then into strips $\frac{1}{4}$in wide and $1\frac{1}{2}$in long. Peel turnips and cut them into strips of the same size.

Select a wide pan which will take all the tournedos steaks comfortably side by side. Pour in well-flavoured beef stock and carrot strips, bring to the boil and simmer for ten minutes. Then add turnips and simmer for five minutes longer.

Meanwhile, wipe or wash mushrooms clean; trim stems. Add them to the simmering pan and continue to cook gently for another five minutes, or until all the vegetables are tender. Drain vegetables and put them aside with a little stock. Return remaining stock to the pan.

Wrap a thin strip of pork fat round the middle of each tournedos. Cut four pieces of string long enough to go round each tournedos and hang over the side of the pan when submerged in stock. Tie one end of each string quite firmly round each tournedos to keep the pork fat in place.

5 Just before serving: bring stock to the boil and lower in tournedos side by side. Simmer for five minutes if you like them rare, eight minutes for medium, and twelve minutes for well done.

6 When tournedos are ready, fish them out by their strings. Drop vegetables into simmering stock to reheat them.

7 Remove strings and strips of pork fat from tournedos and arrange on a shallow, heated serving dish.

8 Season each steak liberally with freshly ground black pepper and sprinkle with a teaspoon of brandy. Garnish the dish with reheated vegetables; moisten them with some of the cooking stock and serve immediately.

Classic beef stock

Makes 3 pints
3lb shin or neck of beef on the bone (see Step 1)
1lb shin of veal on the bone (see Step 1)
1 small ham bone (about ½lb) or ¼lb lean ham
2 Spanish onions, roughly chopped
3 large carrots, roughly chopped
2 leeks, thickly sliced
3–4 stalks celery, thickly sliced
2oz beef dripping
A few mushroom stalks or trimmings
2–3 soft over-ripe tomatoes
Salt
3 sprigs parsley
1 sprig thyme or a pinch of dried thyme
1 bay leaf
1 clove
9 black peppercorns

1 Ask your butcher to remove the meat from the shin (or neck) of beef and shin of veal, and to chop the bones up into large chunks.

2 Preheat oven to very hot (475°F Mark 9).

Trim any excess fat from the meat.

Put beef and veal bones, and the ham in a roasting tin. Add roughly chopped onions and carrots and sliced leeks and celery, and dot with dripping.

Roast bones and vegetables in the oven for forty to forty-five minutes, turning occasionally, until richly browned.

Scrape contents of roasting tin into a large saucepan, casserole or stock-pot. Add boned meat, ham, mushroom stalks or trimmings and soft tomatoes.

Add ½ pint cold water to roasting tin; bring it to the boil, scraping bottom and sides of tin with a wooden spoon to dislodge all the crusty bits and sediment stuck there. Pour over vegetables, and then add 5½ pints cold water.

Place pan over a low heat and bring to the boil. Allow foam to settle into a scum on the surface; skim it off with a slotted spoon, then add a little salt (not too much – remember stock will reduce), which will draw out more scum. Skim again.

When all the scum has been drawn out of the meat and bones, throw in herbs, bay leaf, clove and black peppercorns, and leave stock to simmer gently for three hours.

Strain stock through a fine sieve into a large bowl and allow to cool before skimming off fat. Store until ready to be used.

Note: Meat can be eaten with coarse salt and freshly ground black pepper, or combined with fresh vegetables to make another portion of stock.

Poule au pot à la Béarnaise

Serves 6
A plump boiling fowl, about 5lb, with giblets
Bouquet garni (parsley, celery, bay leaves)
1 onion, stuck with 2 cloves

1 clove garlic, crushed
3 large carrots
3 turnips, halved
4 leeks, white parts only
1 stalk celery
Salt and freshly ground black pepper
1 large, firm cabbage
3 large potatoes, halved

Stuffing
The chicken giblets
2 (extra) chicken livers
6oz lean veal or chicken meat
6oz unsmoked streaky bacon
4oz cooked ham
6oz stale white breadcrumbs
Milk
2 Spanish onions, finely chopped
3 level tablespoons butter
2 level tablespoons finely chopped parsley
2 tablespoons brandy or armagnac
$\frac{1}{4}$ level teaspoon ground allspice
Salt and freshly ground black pepper
1 egg
3 level tablespoons double cream

1 To make stuffing: mince chicken giblets together with 2 extra
   chicken livers, the veal or chicken meat, bacon and ham. Put into
   a large bowl and blend together.

2 Soak breadcrumbs in milk for ten minutes; then squeeze out as
   much moisture as possible.

3 Sauté finely chopped onions in butter over a moderate heat for
   five to six minutes, or until soft but not coloured.

4 Combine sautéed onions and soaked breadcrumbs with minced
   meat mixture and mix again, adding finely chopped parsley,
   brandy or armagnac, allspice, and salt and freshly ground black
   pepper, to taste.

5 Beat egg with cream; add to the bowl and blend until stuffing is smooth and homogeneous.

6 Stuff cavity of boiling fowl with half the mixture and sew up all the openings with a needle and strong thread.

7 Pour 4 pints water into a large pan; add bouquet garni, the onion stuck with cloves, crushed garlic, the stuffed chicken, and all the vegetables except cabbage and potatoes. Season to taste with salt and freshly ground black pepper; bring to the boil over a gentle heat, skimming off scum. If chicken is not totally submerged in liquid, cover protruding part with buttered greaseproof paper. Cover pan tightly and simmer as gently as possible for two hours.

8 In the meantime, bring another large pan of water to the boil and plunge in the cabbage, head downwards. Cover and simmer for seven to ten minutes; then drain and remove six of the best outer leaves. Rinse them in cold water and lay them out flat to drain on a clean cloth or paper towels.

9 Divide remaining stuffing between the leaves. Fold over sides of each leaf and roll up tightly. Wind a thin string round each cabbage roll to prevent it coming apart.

10 When chicken has been simmering for about one and three-quarter hours, add cabbage rolls to the pan.

11 Quarter the cabbage heart and add it to the pan at the end of the two hours' cooking time, together with potatoes, and continue to cook gently for twenty-five to thirty minutes longer, or until potatoes and cabbage are tender but not disintegrating, and chicken is cooked through but still juicy.

12 To serve: remove cabbage rolls from pan with a slotted spoon, taking great care not to crush them, and arrange them to one side on a large, heated serving platter. Lay the chicken in the centre of the dish, and surround with carrots, turnips, potatoes and cabbage wedges. The deliciously rich stock will probably require skimming of excess fat, and can be served before the chicken.

Stuffed whole cabbage

Serves 4–6

1 large Savoy cabbage
Salt
1 tablespoon oil
4 level tablespoons butter
1 Spanish onion, finely chopped
1lb cooked ham, chopped
½lb button mushrooms, chopped
3 level tablespoons long-grain rice, boiled and drained
2 level tablespoons finely chopped red pepper
1 level teaspoon dried oregano
1–2 level tablespoons finely grated Cheddar cheese
Juice of ½ lemon
Freshly ground black pepper

A whole cabbage scooped out and stuffed with a mixture of ham and mushrooms flavoured with onion, oregano and grated Cheddar. Serve with a simple, fresh-tasting tomato sauce and floury boiled potatoes.

1 Remove outer leaves of cabbage and, with a sharp knife, cut out a hole in the top of the cabbage about 4in in diameter. Scoop out centre to about three-quarters of its depth.

2 Bring a large pan of salted water to the boil. Plunge cabbage in it and simmer, covered, for five to ten minutes, making sure that the hole in the centre is filled with water. Drain thoroughly.

3 Heat oil with half the butter in a heavy pan; add finely chopped onion and sauté over a moderate heat for eight to ten minutes until soft and golden brown. Stir in chopped ham and mushrooms, cooked rice and finely chopped red pepper; sprinkle with oregano, mix well and cook over a moderate heat, stirring occasionally, for seven to ten minutes longer, to allow flavours to blend.

4 Add grated Cheddar and lemon juice to the mixture; mix well and season to taste with salt and freshly ground black pepper.

Pile mixture into the hollowed-out cabbage. Dot top with remaining butter and cover with a piece of foil.

Fit a colander (or a large sieve) over a pan of water. Bring to a fast boil; place cabbage in the colander; cover pan and steam for twenty to twenty-five minutes, or until cabbage is cooked through but still very firm. Serve immediately.

New England boiled dinner

Serves 8–10
5lb corned brisket of beef
1lb salt pork
3 bay leaves
6 black peppercorns
1 small boiling fowl, about 4lb
12 large carrots, scraped
6 medium-sized onions, peeled
6 large potatoes, peeled
3 medium-sized turnips, peeled and quartered
1 medium-sized cabbage, quartered
Horseradish chantilly (p.166)

Wipe corned beef with a damp cloth; tie into shape and put into a large stockpot or heavy saucepan. Cover with cold water and bring to the boil; drain and rinse beef. Repeat this operation.

Cover brisket with fresh boiling water; add salt pork, bay leaves and peppercorns; cover and simmer over the lowest heat possible for three to four hours, or until meat is tender, adding chicken after the first hour.

Cool pot slightly; skim excess fat and add carrots, onions, potatoes and turnips. Cook for about twenty minutes, then add cabbage wedges; cook until all the vegetables are tender but not disintegrating – cabbage should remain on the crisp side.

Serve meats on a platter, garnished with pot vegetables. Accompany with *horseradish chantilly*.

Horseradish Chantilly

6–8 tablespoons double cream
1–2 level tablespoons freshly grated raw horseradish
Pinch of salt

1 Whip double cream until it holds shape in soft peaks. Add 1 to 2
tablespoons iced water and whisk until thick and light again.

2 Fold in freshly grated horseradish to taste, and season with a pinch
of salt.

Olla podrida
(Spanish boiled dinner with chick peas)

Serves 5–6
½lb stewing beef
½lb lean leg of lamb
½lb gammon
3 tablespoons olive oil
3 medium-sized Spanish onions
2 cloves garlic, finely chopped
1 small green pepper, seeded, cored and diced
½ level teaspoon turmeric
1½lb boiling chicken joints
1 large stalk celery, coarsely chopped
Bouquet garni (3 sprigs parsley, 1 sprig thyme, 1 bay leaf)
1 chicken stock cube
Salt and freshly ground black pepper
½lb Spanish *chorizo* sausages, skinned and sliced ½in thick
2–3 large ripe tomatoes, peeled and seeded
1lb chick peas, soaked overnight
3 potatoes, peeled and quartered
6 baby carrots, scraped, topped and tailed
½lb French beans, trimmed and cut into 2in lengths
½ small head firm cabbage, cut into 6 wedges

1 Trim beef, lamb and gammon of excess fat, and cut them into
1in cubes.

In a large frying pan, brown beef and lamb cubes thoroughly on all sides in olive oil, a portion at a time so that pan is not overcrowded. Remove meat cubes to a plate with a slotted spoon.

Chop 2 onions coarsely. Add them to the fat remaining in the frying-pan, together with finely chopped garlic and diced green pepper.

Sprinkle with turmeric and sauté over a moderate heat until vegetables are soft and lightly coloured, ten to fifteen minutes. Remove from heat.

Rinse chicken joints and place them in a large pot or deep casserole. Cover with 2¼ pints water. Add remaining onion, quartered, chopped celery, bouquet garni, stock cube, and salt and freshly ground black pepper, to taste.

Place pot over a low heat and slowly bring to simmering point, skimming off scum as it rises to the surface. As soon as liquid simmers, remove pan from heat.

Add browned beef and lamb, gammon, sliced *chorizo*, the contents of the frying-pan, tomatoes and the well-drained chick peas. Mix well.

Return pot to a low heat and very slowly bring it to simmering point again. Regulate heat so that liquid in pot barely bubbles; cover and continue to cook very gently for one hour, or until meats are just tender. If pot is allowed to come to a rolling boil at any time, meats will turn tough and stringy.

Add quartered potatoes and whole carrots, and continue to simmer very gently for a further fifteen minutes.

Finally, add French beans and cabbage wedges, and continue to simmer for twenty minutes, or until all the vegetables are cooked and meats are very tender indeed.

To serve: drain off stock into another pan. Correct seasoning; bring to the boil and serve about three-quarters of it as a soup in deep bowls.

12 Pile meats, chick peas and vegetables on a large, heated serving dish, grouping them attractively. Moisten with remaining stock and serve as the main course.

Couscous

Serves 6

One 3–3½lb roasting chicken
Salt and freshly ground black pepper
3 tablespoons olive oil
2 level teaspoons paprika
1 level teaspoon ground ginger
½ level teaspoon ground cinnamon
¼ level teaspoon saffron strands
2 chicken stock cubes
2 level tablespoons tomato concentrate
1lb packaged *couscous* (see note)
4 level tablespoons chopped parsley
2 level tablespoons butter
Ground ginger, cayenne and tomato concentrate, to finish sauce

Bouquet garni
1 stalk celery, cut into 1in lengths
6 black peppercorns
3 cloves
1 bay leaf
1 clove garlic, peeled
½–1 level teaspoon cumin seed

Vegetables
1 Spanish onion, diced
4 small turnips, diced
½lb carrots, diced
2 medium-sized green peppers, seeded, cored and cut into large dice
4oz chick peas, soaked overnight
One 8oz packet frozen broad beans

The famous dish that goes under the name of *couscous* is composed of two distinct parts: the *couscous* or grain itself, and the stew of fish, meat or poultry over which it steams, and whose flavours it is intended to absorb.

A special pot, known in French-speaking North Africa as a *couscousière*, is used to make it, but you can substitute a saucepan with a steamer and a bowl, both of which fit snugly over the top.

Until the last few years, *couscous* would have been quite impractical for the European kitchen as the grain demands a great deal of tedious and highly expert pre-preparation before it will separate to light fluffiness when cooked. Nowadays, though, the grain is exported ready for its final steaming, which is child's play.

Here is a version of *couscous* with chicken. You can also add shoulder of lamb, cut into serving portions, if you wish.

Cut chicken in half and season with salt and freshly ground black pepper.

Collect ingredients for bouquet garni and tie them up in a square of muslin.

Select a large saucepan, and a steamer which will fit over it tightly, (see introductory note). Heat 2 tablespoons olive oil in it and sauté chicken halves steadily until golden brown all over, ten to fifteen minutes. Transfer chicken halves to a plate.

In the same oil, sauté diced onion, turnips, carrots and green peppers for fifteen minutes, or until golden. Sprinkle with paprika, ginger, cinnamon and saffron, and mix well.

Pour over 2 pints boiling water; add stock cubes, tomato concentrate, bouquet garni, chicken and soaked chick peas. Bring to the boil, reduce heat to a gentle simmer; cover and cook gently for ten minutes.

Meanwhile, prepare *couscous*: place the grain in a bowl and moisten with 6 tablespoons cold water, one at a time, working it in evenly with your fingertips, rather as though you were rubbing fat into flour to make a pastry. The grain will absorb this water without any trouble, and look and feel almost as it did when it came out of the packet.

7 Line steamer with a clean tea cloth (wrung out of boiling water just in case any trace of detergent remains). Place *couscous* in this.

8 Remove lid from pan in which chicken is simmering. Fit steamer over the top and continue to simmer gently, uncovered. Steam *couscous* in this way for thirty minutes, occasionally drawing a fork through the grains to aerate them and ensure that they do not stick together in lumps.

9 After thirty minutes, remove *couscous* from steamer. Spoon grain into a heatproof bowl that will fit snugly over the pan. Sprinkle with remaining tablespoon of olive oil and gradually add a further 6 tablespoons cold water, working it in evenly as before. Season to taste with salt.

10 Add frozen broad beans to stew. Stir in chopped parsley. Fit bowl over the pan; cover bowl with lid and continue to simmer for a further thirty minutes.

11 Add butter to *couscous* and leave to melt while you finish sauce.

12 Strain off ¾ pint liquid from stew. Pour into a small pan. Flavour with a further ¼ level teaspoon ground ginger, a pinch of cayenne and a teaspoon of tomato concentrate. Taste and adjust flavourings/seasonings – sauce should be quite strong. Reheat to boiling point.

13 Toss *couscous* with a fork to mix in melted butter. Heap it around the sides of a large, oval, heated serving platter.

14 Place chicken pieces in the centre. Spoon over as much of the vegetables and juices that your dish will take and serve immediately, handing sauce round separately. Any remaining vegetables and juices can be kept hot in reserve to reinforce the dish if necessary.

Minced meat loaves

Minced meat dishes started off as a clever way of dealing with tough meat in the days when practically all meat was tough. And it is significant to note that meat balls and patties, sauces, and stuffings made with minced meat are still a staple part of the diet in the poorer countries of the world: think of the Mediterranean, for example, and the countries of North Africa.

On the other hand, the steak-loving Americans have developed the hamburger and the baked meat loaf to a fine art. Is this, I wonder, something they have learnt from their immigrants – hamburgers from Hamburg, sauced meat balls from the Mediterranean, and so on?

So much for the past. What *has* changed is the ease with which meat loaves and meat balls can be prepared. With an electric mincer or blender, the actual preparation time is literally reduced to minutes. And they *still* make about the most economical meat dish you could hope to have.

The texture of a meat loaf is a matter of taste. Some prefer a rougher mixture which still has a little bite. And a hamburger should always be coarsely ground. In this case use the coarse blade of your mincer. Others like a super-smooth texture, which can be achieved by dropping cubes of meat, a few at a time, on to turning blades, and blending away until the right consistency is reached.

Mixing of the meats and aromatics can be done right in the blender, or in an electric mixer, but I prefer to work it with my hands, which gives me the best idea of whether the mixture is wet enough.

Moistening the mixture. The most common mistake people make is not using enough liquid in a meat loaf mixture, with the result that the baked loaf is dry. In the majority of cases, the mixture should tend towards the sloppy when raw. Don't be afraid to add a cupped handful of water, or better still, stock, if towards the end of mixing the mixture still feels a little on the dry side.

Shaping patties and meat balls This again is best done by hand. If you have been mixing by hand as well, wash your hands carefully, but leave them thoroughly wet. Scoop up a portion of the mixture and lightly roll or pat into the required shape. Drop straight on to the flour or breadcrumbs with which the patty is to be coated. If, after shaping several patties, the mixture starts to stick to your hands again, simply rinse well and moisten with more water.

Flavouring the raw mixture. Unless it contains pork, go ahead and *taste* it. But if that makes you feel squeamish, a more laborious way is to sauté off a small ball of the mixture in a little butter and oil. Sometimes, the taste of a meat mixture doesn't quite seem to 'jell'. Reach for a bottle of ketchup or tomato purée or Worcestershire sauce, or Tabasco, or try a little French mustard or garlic salt, and see if that makes a difference. It will, but if by chance it doesn't, sauté your onions to a deeper colour next time.

A combination of meats can give a very successful flavour. You can use two kinds, or even three together, chosen from beef, lamb, veal and pork, the last two tending to 'lighten' taste and texture, but remember that *one* of them should always predominate in a (maximum) ratio of 2 : 1.

Blender meat loaf

Serves 6–8

2 eggs
1lb lean beef, minced
½lb lean pork, minced
½lb streaky bacon, chopped
2 level tablespoons tomato concentrate
1 teaspoon Worcestershire sauce

½ level teaspoon oregano or marjoram
Generous pinch of thyme
3 drops Tabasco
1 Spanish onion, finely chopped
1–2 level tablespoons finely chopped parsley
2 slices bread, soaked in chicken stock (not squeezed)
Salt and freshly ground black pepper

A trouble-free dish for a Sunday supper. You can serve the meat loaf *au naturel*, with its cooking juices, or make a simple tomato sauce to go with it. If the container of your blender is not very large, blend the mixture in two stages, then mix thoroughly in a bowl.

Preheat oven to slow (325°F Mark 3).

2 Put eggs in the container of an electric blender. Start blending at low speed, dropping beef, pork and bacon gradually on to turning blades. Then turn up speed to high and continue to blend until smooth.

3 Add remaining ingredients, seasoning generously with salt and freshly ground black pepper, and continue to blend until flavourings are thoroughly incorporated.

Press mixture into a 2lb loaf tin and bake for forty-five minutes to one hour, or until loaf is cooked through and firm to the touch.

When ready to serve, drain off juices into a small pan; skim off as necessary, and keep hot while you slice loaf thickly. Arrange in overlapping slices on a heated serving dish; pour over hot juices and serve immediately.

Meat loaf in shirtsleeves

Serves 4

Meat loaf
Butter
1 Spanish onion, finely chopped
3 slices stale white bread cut from a large loaf

$\frac{1}{4}$ pint beef stock (p.160)
$\frac{3}{4}$lb lean minced beef
$\frac{1}{4}$lb lean minced pork
2 level tablespoons finely chopped parsley
$\frac{1}{2}$ level teaspoon mixed herbs
1 egg, beaten
1 teaspoon Worcestershire sauce
Dash of Tabasco
$\frac{1}{2}$ level teaspoon salt
Freshly ground black pepper

To wrap in 'shirtsleeves'
8oz frozen puff pastry, defrosted
3 level tablespoons French mustard
Beaten egg, to glaze

For best results, make the meat loaf first thing in the morning of the day you intend to serve it, or even the night before, so that it will be quite cold and firm before you attempt to wrap it in pastry.

1 Preheat oven to fairly hot (425°F Mark 7).

2 Grease a 1lb loaf tin generously with butter.

3 To make *meat loaf*: simmer finely chopped onion in 2 level tablespoons butter over a low heat until very soft and golden but not brown, ten to fifteen minutes.

4 Trim crusts from bread slices. In a large bowl, soak bread slices in beef stock for ten minutes; then shred to a pulp with a fork.

5 Add remaining ingredients to bowl, including sautéed onion and the butter in which it was cooked; beat with a wooden spoon or knead by hand until thoroughly blended.

6 Pack meat mixture into prepared loaf tin and level off with a spatula or the back of a spoon. Cover tin tightly with foil.

7 Bake meat loaf for forty-five minutes. Remove from oven and leave to become quite cold, covered, before wrapping 'in shirtsleeves'.

8 When ready to proceed, preheat oven to moderately hot (400°F Mark 6).

9 Roll puff pastry into a 12in square.

10 Turn meat loaf out of its tin. Scrape off any excess fat and spread exposed surfaces with 2 level tablespoons mustard.

11 Set meat loaf in the centre of the pastry square with the remaining unspread surface upwards (use two forks to lift the loaf). Spread with remaining mustard.

12 Wrap meat loaf up in pastry like a parcel, sealing edges with a little beaten egg and trimming off excess pastry. Cut out small vents in the centre top to allow steam to escape. Decorate with leaves and tassels made from trimmings. Brush pastry all over with beaten egg.

13 Transfer pastry-wrapped meat loaf to an ungreased baking sheet and bake for thirty minutes, or until pastry is crisply puffed and a rich golden colour all over.

14 Serve hot, cut into thick slices, and if you wish, accompanied by a simple tomato sauce.

Cumberland pork loaf

Serves 6
2oz fresh white breadcrumbs
$\frac{1}{4}$ pint milk
$1\frac{1}{2}$lb lean minced pork
$\frac{1}{2}$lb pork sausage meat
1 egg, lightly beaten
Salt and freshly ground black pepper
2 bay leaves
Finely chopped parsley, to garnish

Cumberland topping
4 level tablespoons redcurrant jelly
4 level tablespoons Demerara sugar
Finely grated rind of 1 orange

2 tablespoons orange juice or 1 tablespoon each orange juice
and port
2 level teaspoons French mustard

1 Preheat oven to moderate (350°F Mark 4).

2 Leave breadcrumbs to soak in milk until needed.

3 Blend Cumberland topping ingredients together. Spread over the
base of a 2lb loaf tin.

4 In a large bowl, combine minced pork, sausage meat, soaked
breadcrumbs, together with any milk left unabsorbed, and lightly
beaten egg. Blend thoroughly by hand or with a wooden spoon.
Season with at least 1 level teaspoon salt and freshly ground black
pepper, to taste.

5 Spoon meat mixture carefully over topping, which is very wet,
tapping tin firmly several times to settle mixture and eliminate air
pockets. Level off top with the back of the spoon. Lay bay leaves
on surface.

6 Cover tin tightly with foil.

7 Bake loaf for one hour.

8 To serve: allow meat loaf to 'settle' for a few minutes. Then
remove bay leaves and invert loaf carefully on to a heated serving
dish, which should be curved to contain the sauce created by the
topping mixture. Garnish with finely chopped parsley and serve
immediately.

Liver and sausage luncheon loaf

Serves 6
Butter
1½lb beef liver
1 small onion, peeled and quartered
1 clove garlic, crushed
3oz trimmed white bread

12oz pork sausage meat
1 egg, lightly beaten
2 level tablespoons finely chopped parsley
1 level tablespoon tomato ketchup
1 teaspoon Worcestershire sauce
Dash of Tabasco
Salt and freshly ground black pepper
4 level tablespoons stale white breadcrumbs

1 Grease a 2lb loaf tin generously with butter and line base with buttered greaseproof paper.

2 Preheat oven to moderate (350°F Mark 4).

3 Put liver, onion and garlic through the standard blade of a mincer. 'Chase' them through with the bread.

4 Add sausage meat, the egg, parsley, ketchup, Worcestershire sauce and Tabasco, and beat with a wooden spoon until smoothly blended. Mixture should be rather loose.

5 Season with about 1 level teaspoon salt and freshly ground black pepper to taste. (Bought sausage meat is usually seasoned already.)

6 Pack mixture in loaf tin. Level off top with the back of a spoon. Sprinkle surface evenly with breadcrumbs.

7 Bake loaf for one and a quarter hours.

8 Remove from oven and allow to 'rest' for ten minutes before turning out on to a heated serving dish. Serve immediately.

Note: A light mushroom, mustard or onion sauce makes a pleasant accompaniment.

Hamburgers

Makes 1 hamburger

Recipe I
4oz lean steak, coarsely minced

1 level teaspoon finely chopped parsley
1 level teaspoon finely chopped onion
Salt and freshly ground black pepper

Recipe II
4oz lean steak, coarsely minced
1 teaspoon tomato ketchup
¼ teaspoon Worcestershire sauce
Salt and freshly ground black pepper

Recipe III
4oz lean steak, coarsely minced
¼ teaspoon soy sauce
2 drops Tabasco
Salt and freshly ground black pepper

Try these hamburgers, then let your imagination run riot with different flavourings and seasonings. Do not mince the meat too finely or the hamburgers will lose their succulent, crumbly texture.

1 Preheat grill to very hot.

2 With a fork, mix minced meat with seasonings, adding salt and freshly ground black pepper to taste. Shape lightly into a round, about ¾in thick.

3 Sprinkle grill-pan with salt (or place a piece of foil on rack of grill pan and sprinkle that with salt). Place hamburger on top and grill for about three minutes on each side. Serve immediately, with cooking juices spooned over the hamburgers.

Albóndigas
Spanish meat balls

Serves 4–6
½lb minced beef
½lb minced veal
1lb minced pork
½lb streaky bacon, minced
4 level tablespoons fresh white breadcrumbs
4 tablespoons milk
1 Spanish onion, finely chopped

Olive oil
1 level teaspoon salt
$\frac{1}{2}$ level teaspoon dried thyme
$\frac{1}{4}$ level teaspoon cayenne pepper
Grated rind of $\frac{1}{2}$ lemon
2 eggs, beaten
Tomato sauce, to serve

These meat balls are a popular dish in Spain, Portugal and many of the South American countries. Here is one version.

1 Put minced meats in a large mixing bowl.

2 Soak breadcrumbs in milk.

3 Sauté finely chopped onion in 2 tablespoons olive oil until soft and golden. Add to minced meats and mix well.

4 Add soaked breadcrumbs, salt, thyme, cayenne pepper, lemon rind and beaten eggs. Knead thoroughly by hand or mix with a wooden spoon until mixture is smooth and ingredients are well blended. Refrigerate for thirty minutes.

5 When meat mixture is firm, shape it into walnut-sized balls. Sauté gently in a little olive oil until meat balls are cooked through and a rich golden brown, about fifteen minutes.

6 Serve hot with a rich tomato sauce.

Lesson 6

Deep-frying potatoes and other vegetables

In many homes, deep-frying is a thing of the past. Cooks are reluctant to attempt it on their home ground, knowing full well that without adequate ventilation the whole house is liable to reek of fat. Unless your kitchen is equipped with a powerful extractor or you can keep the kitchen door shut and the window wide open while you work, you may be forgiven if you don't care to deep-fry when you're all dressed up for a formal dinner party. But please don't let this deter you from treating your family to crisp fritters and *beignets*, and nutty, home-made potato chips on less formal occasions.

Deep-frying equipment

For easy, foolproof deep-frying, you should equip yourself with a large deep-frying pan and frying basket, and a thermometer for measuring the temperature of the fat or oil. However, you can start out without either of these if necessary.

Deep-frying pan Provided you have a large, wide, heavy saucepan with a flat base that sits securely on the hob, a long handle and a well-fitting lid to clamp on in case the fat catches fire, you are ready to go. Instead of the frying-basket, have a large slotted spoon to fish out the food when it's ready. Then, if deep-frying appeals to you, get a proper deep-fryer. It is much more convenient to use (a) because of the frying-basket, and (b) because the fat can be left in it between reasonably frequent frying sessions.

Fat thermometer A thermometer for measuring the temperature of fat, sugar syrups, etc. is an invaluable piece of equipment to have around in the kitchen. In deep-frying, the temperature of the fat is probably the one most important factor: too hot, and the food will set and burn on the surface before it has had a chance to puff up and cook (or reheat) all the way through; not hot enough, and the surface will not be sealed quickly with the result that the fritter will be sodden with fat.

Until you get a proper thermometer, use the bread test to determine the temperature of the fat: cut a 1in cube of day-old bread. When you think the fat is hot enough, drop it in. The table below gives, roughly, the time it will take for the bread cube to turn crisp and golden brown:

350°F   90 seconds
375°F   60 seconds
425°F   30 seconds

Fat for deep-frying

You can choose between lard, olive oil and one of the anonymous vegetable oils now on the market. *Lard* contributes more richness of flavour than any of the others, and I prefer it above all for doughnuts, sweet fritters and deep-fried pastries. *Olive oil* imparts a characteristic nutty flavour – some people love it, others dislike it intensely. If you enjoy the food of the Mediterranean, you will like to try potato chips, vegetables and fish deep-fried in olive oil. *Vegetable oils* are for dishes where you want no interference in the flavour of the food itself.

Butter and margarine are useless for deep-frying. Their burning point is way below the 375°F usually required for deep-frying.

Regulating the temperature One of the trickiest parts about deep-frying is keeping the temperature of the fat or oil steady once you have heated it to the required level. If you're not careful, the temperature will continue to rise. In extreme cases, you can lower it quickly and efficiently by adding a lump of cold lard to the pan, or pouring in more cold oil. If you realise it in time, though, you can draw the pan to one side and carry on frying *off* the heat until the temperature settles down again.

A drastic drop in temperature may be caused if you attempt to deep-fry too many chips or fritters at one time. Avoid this either by frying them in small batches, or by turning up the heat briefly as soon as they go in.

Storing fat or oil There is no need to discard the fat (or oil) used after each session provided you filter out all the impurities before putting it away. If you keep adding more fresh fat (or oil) to the current batch, you will find this makes it last much longer. The fat should be discarded once it discolours badly, smells less than fresh and develops a tendency to smoke at a moderate temperature (375°F).

Rules for deep-frying

1 Never leave a pan of fat or oil to heat unattended. If it overheats, it will at best acquire a nasty, burnt flavour and have to be discarded, at worst catch fire.

2 Make sure that the level of the fat leaves at least 2½in clear at the top of the pan. There is always a certain amount of frothing when the food is added, and if the fat spills over, it may cause a nasty fire. On the other hand, the *minimum* depth of oil or fat you can deep-fry in is between 2in and 3in.

3 Because of points 1 and 2 above, always have a metal lid near at hand so that if the fat does catch fire, you can quickly contain it by depriving the flames of oxygen. *Never* try to extinguish a burning pan of fat with water.

4 Make sure that the thermometer and any spoons, etc. that come in contact with the hot oil are perfectly dry. Water causes the oil to spit viciously and you could give yourself a nasty burn.

5 For the same reason, carefully dry off uncoated (i.e. unbattered) food, chips for example, before adding them to the pan.

6 Don't fry too many fritters, or whatever, at a time. As we have already pointed out, this is likely to cause a sharp fall in temperature,

and it may also result in fritters sticking together as they puff up. There should be enough room for the whole batch to bob about freely on the surface without getting in each others' way.

7 Recheck the temperature of the fat frequently.

8 Drain deep-fried morsels thoroughly on a bed of crumpled absorbent paper and *serve them immediately* as they rapidly lose their crispness.

Chips with everything

Follow the simple rules below and limp, sodden chips will be a thing of the past.

* Use plenty of fat for frying chips – 3 pints should be enough for up to 2lb potatoes – so that they don't crowd and stick together.

* Dripping, lard or vegetable oil can all be used. Olive oil gives a distinct and delicious flavour all of its own. Make sure your fat is fresh and sweet, and don't hesitate to throw it out if you suspect that it's going rancid.

* Use a proper deep-frying pan with a basket, and make sure it is large enough for your needs: the level of the fat should be at least 2½in below the top of the pan, otherwise it may froth up over the top, and then you're in real trouble. (If the pan does catch fire, clap on a lid as quickly as you can, or failing that, cover the top completely with a heavy baking sheet to cut out the oxygen.)

* Chipped potatoes should always be rinsed thoroughly to remove excess starch from the surface, then dried carefully with a cloth. This is crucial not only for the sake of safety, but also because excess moisture would lower the heat of the fat as it evaporates and cause the chips to become saturated.

* Be very careful when you lower the basket of potatoes into the pan. There will inevitably be a certain amount of spitting and foaming, so stand well back.

* Finely cut potatoes such as game chips, *pommes allumettes* and *pommes pailles* should be cooked a handful at a time to give them plenty of room, and also because they tend to froth more vigorously.

* English chips and French fries are cooked in two stages. The first of these, which leaves the chips soft but still very pale, can be done well in advance (the same day, of course); the second stage takes place just before serving so that the chips come hot and crisp to the table. Always make sure that the second frying temperature is appreciably higher than the first. If it is not, your chips will be drunk with fat.

* Have by you plenty of crumpled absorbent paper. As soon as the chips are cooked, tip them out on to the paper to drain thoroughly. Serve immediately with a light sprinkling of salt.

Chips – English style

Serves 4–6
2lb medium-sized potatoes
3 pints fat or oil for deep-frying (see above)
Salt

1 Peel potatoes. Wash them and cut them lengthwise into slices $\frac{1}{2}$in thick. Then cut each slice lengthwise into sticks $\frac{1}{2}$in wide. Rinse potato sticks thoroughly under the cold tap to rid them of their surface starch and dry carefully with a clean cloth.

2 In a deep-frying pan, heat fat or oil to 350°F, or until a cube of bread dropped into it browns within ninety seconds. Lower heat to keep temperature steady.

3 Place potato sticks in the frying-basket. Lower them gently into the fat, at the same time raising the heat under the pan for a minute or two to compensate for the temperature loss that this will have caused.

4 Deep-fry potatoes for five minutes, or until soft but still pale.

5 Lift out the basket. Shake it lightly over the pan to get rid of the worst of the excess oil; then tip the chips out on to absorbent paper and drain thoroughly. (If chips are not to be given their second frying for some time, wrap them loosely in greaseproof paper and put aside.)

6 When chips are required, reheat pan of fat or oil to 425°F, or until a fresh bread cube browns in thirty seconds.

7 Return chips to frying basket; lower them into the hot fat, raising the heat as before to maintain the temperature. Fry chips for two minutes, or until crisp and golden.

8 Tip chips out on to fresh absorbent paper. Drain thoroughly and serve at once, sprinkled with salt.

Chips – French style

Cut peeled potatoes lengthwise into slices $\frac{1}{3}$in thick, then into sticks $\frac{1}{3}$in wide. Proceed as above but give potato sticks three minutes' frying instead of five the first time around.

Pommes allumettes

Cut peeled potatoes into slices $\frac{1}{8}$in thick, then into sticks $\frac{1}{8}$in wide. Wash and dry as above. Deep-fry once only, at 425°F, for two to three minutes, or until crisp and golden.

Pommes pailles

Cut peeled potatoes into slices $\frac{1}{16}$in thick (paper-thin), then into fine strips, or use a special cutter. Wash and dry as above. Deep-fry once only, at 425°F, for about two minutes, or until crisp and golden.

Crisps (game chips)

Cut peeled potatoes into slices $\frac{1}{16}$in thick (paper-thin), or use a mandolin cutter if you have one. Wash and dry as above. Deep-fry once only, at 425°F, for one to two minutes, or until crisp and golden.

185

Pommes soufflées

It would be dishonest of me to pretend that these crisp, puffed little pillows are easy to make. Luck plays a part in it, as well as the type of potato used, and even professional chefs admit to a high failure rate – i.e. of 'pillows' that have declined to puff.

The best potatoes to use are old, red-skinned ones. New potatoes don't work.

The theory is simple enough: potatoes are cut into slices $\frac{1}{8}$in thick, then trimmed into little oval pillows about 2in long and $\frac{3}{4}$in wide. Don't rinse them.

Deep-fry a small portion at a time at 275°F for two minutes only until soft but not at all coloured. Drain and cool.

For the second frying, preheat fat or oil to 475°F. It is the sudden shock of this high temperature that turns the moisture left inside the pillows to steam and – in theory – puffs them up. Lower in the basket and turn the little pillows about gently with a slotted spoon so that they cook evenly.

Drain on absorbent paper and serve immediately – and console yourself with the fact that any pillows which have not puffed up will make excellent crisps.

Deep-fried vegetables
Deep-fried aubergines

Serves 4–6
4 large ripe aubergines
Salt and freshly ground black pepper
Plain flour
Olive oil for deep-frying

Serve deep-fried aubergines piping-hot as a summer appetiser, sprinkled with cinnamon and accompanied by a bowl of plain, cool yoghourt. Or, as an accompaniment to grilled meats or poultry. You'll find they are compulsive eating.

1 Wipe aubergines clean and trim off stems.

2 Cut aubergines in thin slices horizontally or vertically, depending on whether they are the long or round variety. Sprinkle with salt and leave in a colander for at least 30 minutes to allow bitter juices to drain away.

3 Rinse aubergine slices thoroughly. Pat them dry with paper towels and dust lightly with seasoned flour.

4 Preheat a pan of olive oil to 375°F.

5 Deep-fry aubergine slices in hot oil for five minutes, or until crisp and golden brown. Drain thoroughly on absorbent paper and serve immediately, otherwise they quickly become limp again.

Deep-fried courgettes

Serves 4–6
8 courgettes
Plain flour
Salt and freshly ground black pepper
Olive oil for deep-frying

Deep-fried courgettes make an excellent accompaniment to grilled meats or poultry.

Wipe courgettes clean and trim off stems.

Cut courgettes in thin rounds or into thin slices horizontally and then into thin strips, and dust lightly with seasoned flour.

Preheat a pan of olive oil to 375°F.

Deep-fry courgette slices or strips in hot oil for four to five minutes, or until crisp and golden brown. Drain thoroughly on absorbent paper and serve immediately.

Batters for vegetables

Fritter batter

Makes $\frac{3}{4}$ pint
4oz plain flour
Pinch of salt
2 tablespoons olive oil
8 tablespoons tepid water
2 egg whites

A light, all-purpose fritter batter.

1 Sift flour and salt into a bowl, and make a well in the centre.

2 Pour in olive oil and 8 tablespoons tepid water, and stir with a wooden spoon, gradually incorporating flour from sides of well until blended to a smooth batter. Leave to rest for thirty minutes.

3 When ready to use batter: whisk egg whites until stiff but not dry, and fold in gently but thoroughly. Use immediately.

Light beer batter

Makes $\frac{3}{4}$ pint
5oz plain flour
Pinch of salt
2 tablespoons olive oil
$\frac{1}{4}$ pint beer, preferably lager
1 egg white

1 Sift flour and salt into a bowl, and make a well in the centre.

2 Pour in olive oil and gradually add beer, stirring with a wooden spoon to incorporate flour from sides of well. Batter should be completely smooth and slightly thicker than a *crêpe* batter. Leave to rest for two hours.

3 When ready to use batter: whisk egg white until stiff but not dry, and fold in gently but thoroughly. Use immediately.

Deep-fried tomato slices

Serves 4–6
4–8 firm round tomatoes (according to size)
Salt and freshly ground black pepper
Lemon juice
Oil or fat for deep-frying
Fritter or *light beer batter* (p.188)

Choose firm tomatoes; dip them one by one into boiling water
for a second or two and then peel them with a sharp knife.

Cut into thick slices and remove seeds. Place in a bowl and season
with salt, freshly ground black pepper and a little lemon juice.

Preheat a pan of oil or fat to 375°F.

Dip tomato slices in batter and deep-fry for about three minutes, or
until crisp and golden. Drain thoroughly on absorbent paper and
serve immediately.

Deep-fried onion slices

Serves 4–6
4 medium-sized onions
Milk
Flour
Salt and freshly ground black pepper
Oil or fat for deep-frying

Peel onions and slice thinly. Dip in milk and then in flour which
you have seasoned generously with salt and freshly ground black
pepper.

Preheat a pan of oil or fat to 375°F.

Deep-fry onion slices for about three minutes, or until crisp and
golden. Drain thoroughly on absorbent paper and serve
immediately.

Some deep-fried cooked vegetables

Crisp cooked vegetables – artichoke hearts, Jerusalem artichokes, cauliflower and salsify – make wonderful deep-fried accompaniments to grilled and roast meats and poultry. The secret here is to lightly poach them so that they stay crisp and then to enhance their natural flavour with a little lemon juice, olive oil, parsley, salt and pepper before they are dipped in the batter of your choice and deep-fried until golden.

Here again, a word of warning: only deep-fry batter-dipped cooked vegetables until batter is crisp and golden. That will be enough to make the small amounts of sliced or sectioned vegetables piping hot inside their golden crust.

Deep-fried cauliflowerets

Serves 4–6
1 head of cauliflower, separated into cauliflowerets and
    poached in boiling salted water until just tender
2 level tablespoons finely chopped parsley
4 tablespoons olive oil
Juice of ½ lemon
Salt and freshly ground black pepper
Oil or fat for deep-frying
Batter (p.188)

1 Drain poached cauliflowerets. Transfer them into a bowl and sprinkle with finely chopped parsley, olive oil and lemon juice and salt and freshly ground black pepper, to taste. Toss gently and allow to stand at room temperature for at least thirty minutes to absorb flavours.

2 Preheat a pan of oil or fat to 375°F.

3 Dip flowerets in batter and deep-fry for about three minutes, or until crisp and golden. Drain thoroughly on absorbent paper and serve immediately.

Deep-fried artichoke hearts

Serves 4–6

6 large fresh artichoke hearts, poached in salted boiling water
   until just tender (or 8 canned artichoke hearts)
$\frac{1}{2}$ clove garlic, finely chopped
Juice of $\frac{1}{2}$ lemon
Salt and freshly ground black pepper
Oil or fat for deep-frying
Batter (p.188)

1 Drain artichoke hearts thoroughly. Then slice them into thick
   strips. Sprinkle strips with finely chopped garlic, lemon juice and
   salt and freshly ground black pepper to taste. Toss gently and allow
   to stand at room temperature for at least thirty minutes to absorb
   flavours.

2 Preheat pan of oil or fat to 375°F.

3 Dip artichoke strips in batter and deep-fry for about three minutes,
   or until crisp and golden. Drain thoroughly on absorbent paper and
   serve immediately.

Deep-fried Jerusalem artichokes

Serves 4–6

1lb Jerusalem artichokes, trimmed and poached in salted
   boiling water until just tender
Lemon juice
Oil or fat for deep-frying
Salt and freshly ground black pepper
Batter (p.188)

Drain Jerusalem artichokes and cut into thick slices. Sprinkle slices
with a little lemon juice and olive oil and season generously with
salt and freshly ground black pepper. Toss gently and allow to
stand at room temperature for at least thirty minutes to absorb
flavours.

Preheat a pan of oil or fat to 375°F.

3 Dip artichoke slices in batter and deep-fry for about three minutes, or until crisp and golden. Drain thoroughly on absorbent paper and and serve immediately.

Deep-fried salsify

Serves 4–6
1½–2lb salsify
Lemon juice
Plain flour
Salt and freshly ground black pepper
Olive oil for deep-frying
Lemon quarters

An unusual vegetable which takes well to deep-frying.

1 Wash salsify and scrape them clean, then slice into paper thin rounds. Note: to prevent discolouration after scraping keep salsify in water acidulated with lemon juice.

2 Dust with seasoned flour.

3 Preheat pan of oil to 375°F.

4 Deep-fry salsify slices in hot oil until crisp and golden.

5 Drain thoroughly and serve immediately with lemon quarters.

Lesson 7

American and continental cheesecakes

There are two basic types of cheesecake: the continental, or cooked cheesecake, usually baked in a pastry case of some kind, and the American-inspired 'uncooked' cheesecake, which relies on gelatine instead of flour and/or eggs to set it. Another reliable guide to origin is the preference that Americans have for using crushed biscuits fused together with butter to make the base.

Which cheese to use

American cheesecakes use a lot of *cream cheese*, 'Philadelphia' in particular. This is excellent when you want the cheese to give texture and rely on other ingredients to provide flavour.

My favourite is ordinary *curd cheese*, similar to the French *fromage blanc*. Unfortunately, English curd cheese is often badly drained, and in its bought state contains enough moisture to upset the balance of the remaining ingredients. To counteract this, wrap the cheese tightly in a double thickness of muslin; shape it into a ball and leave it to drain overnight in a colander, heavily weighted with a panful of water or a board topped with as many cans of food as you can muster. You will be surprised by the amount of moisture this will force out of it. The following day, finish the operation by twisting the ends of the muslin and squeezing the ball of cheese until no more beads of moisture spring to the surface.

Unfortunately, curd cheese is still not universally available in this country. A good alternative is *cottage cheese*. This will probably also need draining like curd cheese, though the moisture seems to be easier to extract and may not require the initial overnight draining under weights; then, unless the recipe calls for thorough beating with an electric mixer, rub cottage cheese through a sieve to smooth out the lumps.

Baking a cheesecake

You will notice that most of our cheesecakes, especially those high in egg content, bake slowly. This preserves their smooth, uncurdled texture, stops them cracking on the surface, and also avoids too excessive a rise, which usually results in the cake sinking in the middle as it cools. A tiny amount of flour in the cheese mixture helps to prevent this by strengthening the structure of the cake, but basically, controlled heat is the answer.

If, in spite of these precautions, the cheesecake persists in sinking, then I suspect the cheese has not been drained well enough and the raw mixture has been too liquid for the eggs and flour to be able to set it firmly enough.

American cheesecake with black cherry topping

Makes 8 portions

Biscuit crust
4oz wholemeal biscuits
1 level tablespoon castor sugar
1oz unsalted butter, softened

Cheese filling
1lb curd or cottage cheese
6oz castor sugar
Finely grated rind of 2 lemons
Finely grated rind of 1 orange
3 eggs
1½ level tablespoons self-raising flour
4 level tablespoons double cream

Cherry topping
Two 14oz cans pitted black cherries
1–2 tablespoons lemon juice
1 level teaspoon arrowroot

1 To make biscuit crust: crush biscuits finely or put them through a mincer. Stir in sugar and work in butter until thoroughly dispersed throughout mixture.

2 Press biscuit mixture evenly over the base of a loose-bottomed, 7½in cake tin.

3 Preheat oven to moderately hot (400°F Mark 6).

4 To make cheese filling: if using curd cheese, squeeze it out in a double thickness of muslin to extract as much moisture as possible. If using cottage cheese, rub it through a fine-meshed sieve.

5 Put cheese in a bowl. Add sugar and beat until soft and creamy.

6 Beat in finely grated lemon and orange rinds; then add eggs, one at a time, beating well between each addition.

7 Sift flour into the bowl; add double cream and mix gently just enough to blend in ingredients.

8 Spoon cheese mixture over prepared crust.

9 Bake cheesecake for ten minutes; then reduce heat to very slow (275°F Mark 1) and bake for about two hours, or a little longer, until cake is an even golden colour and feels firm when pressed in the centre.

10 Allow cheesecake to cool in its tin. Chill for three hours, or overnight.

11 To make cherry topping: drain canned cherries, reserving syrup. Pit them if necessary and arrange them tightly side by side on top of the cheesecake.

12 Measure 3 fluid oz cherry syrup into a small pan. Add lemon juice, to taste.

13 Cream arrowroot smoothly with a little of the prepared syrup. Heat remaining syrup and when it is hot, stir in creamed

arrowroot. Bring to the boil, and simmer until glaze is thick and translucent. Cool.

14 Spoon glaze over cherries and return cake to the refrigerator to set before taking it out of its tin.

Apricot cheesecake

Serves 6–8

Crust
6oz digestive biscuits
2oz softened butter

Filling
¾lb ripe fresh apricots, halved and stoned
Two 3oz packets Philadelphia cream cheese
8oz cottage cheese
4 level tablespoons castor sugar
1 teaspoon vanilla essence
Juice and finely grated rind of 1 lemon
2 egg yolks, beaten
1 level tablespoon powdered gelatine
½ pint double cream
2 egg whites

Topping
2oz sugar
1lb fresh apricots, halved and stoned
2 level tablespoons apricot jam, sieved
1 level tablespoon toasted flaked almonds

Canned apricots may be used to make this cheesecake when fresh ones are out of season, but if you do so, you may have to use less sugar (or more lemon) in the cheese filling, and sharpen the flavour of the glaze with a little lemon juice as well.

1 Preheat oven to slow (325°F Mark 3).

2 To make crust: crush biscuits finely and blend with softened butter.

Press mixture evenly into an 8in, loose-bottomed cake tin. Bake for ten minutes; remove from oven and allow to cool.

3 To make filling: put halved, stoned apricots in a pan with $\frac{1}{4}$ pint water; simmer, mashing occasionally with a wooden spoon, until apricots are reduced to a pulp. Cool and drain off excess moisture.

4 Combine cheeses, sugar and vanilla essence in a large bowl. Add lemon juice, grated lemon rind and beaten egg yolks, and whisk until smooth.

5 Soften gelatine in 2 tablespoons cold water in a small cup; then place cup in a bowl of hot water and stir until gelatine has completely dissolved. Add to cheese mixture and blend thoroughly.

6 Whip cream lightly and fold into mixture, together with apricot pulp.

7 Whisk egg whites until stiff but not dry and fold gently into cheese mixture.

8 Spoon cheese mixture over crumb base, and chill in the refrigerator until set.

9 To make topping: dissolve sugar in $\frac{1}{2}$ pint water over a low heat. Poach apricots in this syrup until just cooked, ten to fifteen minutes, depending on ripeness. Drain fruit, reserving syrup; remove skins carefully; pat apricot halves dry and arrange them on top of chilled cheesecake, close together.

10 Add sieved apricot jam to syrup and spoon over top of cheesecake. Sprinkle with toasted flaked almonds. Serve very cold.

Bilberry cheesecake

Serves 6–8

Crust
1lb crushed digestive biscuits
6oz melted butter

¼ level teaspoon cinnamon
Pinch of salt
or
One 9in tart shell, prebaked

Filling
10oz cottage cheese, sieved
2 eggs
½ pint sour cream
4–6 level tablespoons castor sugar
3–4 teaspoons lemon juice
1 teaspoon vanilla essence
3 drops almond essence
Pinch of salt

Topping
One 16oz jar bilberries in light syrup (see note)
1½ level tablespoons cornflour
2 teaspoons lemon juice
Pinch of salt
Pinch of ground cinnamon

Fresh bilberries appear all too briefly in English shops in late summer. However, you can also buy excellent bilberries bottled in light syrup, with a full, fresh flavour (if possible, don't buy a can, where you can't see whether the bilberries are whole as they should be, or all mushed up). Or you can equally well substitute blackcurrants in syrup, which may be easier to track down.

Prepare this cheesecake in your favourite crust – I like a crisp, thin shortcrust shell to act as a foil to the delicate filling, but you may prefer to use a crushed biscuit crust. It should be at least 2in deep to hold the filling comfortably, and baked in a loose-bottomed tin to facilitate removal.

1 Preheat oven to moderate (375°F Mark 5). Leave the baked tart shell in its tin.

2 To make filling: combine sieved cheese with remaining ingredients and beat vigorously with a wooden spoon until smooth

and creamy. (If you have an electric blender, it is not necessary to sieve cheese; simply blend ingredients at speed four for about two minutes, or until smooth.)

Pour filling into prepared shell and bake for forty-five minutes, or until set. Remove from oven and allow to cool completely.

To make topping: drain bilberries. Blend cornflour smoothly with a few tablespoons of the bilberry syrup and combine with remaining syrup in a small, heavy pan.

Cook over a moderate heat, stirring until smooth and thick, about four minutes from the time mixture comes to the boil. Allow to cool. Stir in bilberries and flavour to taste with lemon juice, a tiny pinch of salt and a larger one of cinnamon.

Spoon bilberry topping over cheesecake and chill until firm.

Serve cheesecake very cold, but not chilled, unmoulded on to a flat dish.

German cheesecake

Serves 6–8

Pastry base
6oz plain flour
4oz softened butter
2oz castor sugar
1 egg yolk
$\frac{1}{4}$ level teaspoon finely grated lemon rind

Cheese filling
2oz sultanas
1–2 tablespoons dark rum
12oz cottage cheese
4 eggs, separated
1 level teaspoon finely grated lemon rind
4oz castor sugar
1 level tablespoon plain flour, sifted

1 Preheat oven to slow (325°F Mark 3).

2 To make pastry case: sift flour into a large bowl and make a well in the centre.

3 In another bowl, cream butter and sugar together.

4 When mixture is light and fluffy, blend in the egg yolk and finely grated lemon rind.

5 Finally, work in flour to make a smooth, softish dough.

6 Press dough evenly over the base of a deep, loose-bottomed cake tin 7in in diameter.

7 Bake for twenty minutes until firm but not coloured.

8 Remove pastry base from oven and allow to cool in the tin. At the same time, reduce oven temperature to very slow (275°F Mark 1).

9 To make cheese filling: toss sultanas with rum in a small bowl or cup and leave to macerate until required.

10 Rub cottage cheese through a fine sieve into a large bowl.

11 Beat in egg yolks and finely grated lemon rind until smoothly blended.

12 In another bowl that is perfectly clean and dry, whisk egg whites until stiff but not dry. Then gradually whisk in castor sugar and sifted flour, and continue to whisk to a stiff, glossy meringue.

13 With a large metal spoon or spatula, carefully fold meringue into cheese mixture.

14 Spoon mixture over prebaked pastry case. Sprinkle surface with rum-soaked sultanas.

15 Bake cheesecake for forty to fifty minutes until firm to the touch.

16 Cool; remove from tin and chill lightly before serving.

Viennese cheesecake

Makes 8–10 portions

Pastry base
6oz plain flour
2oz icing sugar
3oz butter, softened
1 egg yolk
2 tablespoons iced water

Cheese filling
One ¼lb curd cheese
5oz butter, softened
5 eggs, separated
7oz icing sugar, sifted
Juice and finely grated rind of 2 lemons
½ teaspoon vanilla essence
1½oz plain flour
2oz raisins or coarsely chopped sultanas
1oz chopped candied peel
Sifted icing sugar or a light lemon water icing, to decorate

The Viennese are possibly the most ardent, as well as the most discriminating cake- and pastry-lovers in Europe. The names of their great pastry-shops or *Konditorei* such as Sacher's and Gerstner's are famous throughout the world. Sharing pride of place with their *Torten*, *Krapfen*, *Stollen*, and other *Kuchen* with equally rich-sounding names, is this cheesecake, lighter than most, yet at the same time as rich in flavour as you could wish.

1 Prepare pastry base: sift flour and icing sugar into a bowl and rub in softened butter with your fingertips until mixture resembles fine breadcrumbs.

2 Make a well in the centre; drop in the egg yolk; sprinkle with iced water and mix together with a fork. Then knead lightly and quickly by hand to make a smooth dough.

3 Roll dough into a ball. Wrap in greaseproof paper and refrigerate for one hour.

4 Preheat oven to moderately hot (400°F Mark 6).

5 Flour a board and rolling pin lightly, and roll dough out ⅛in thick.

6 Line base and sides of a deep, loose-bottomed cake tin 9in in diameter with dough. Prick all over with a fork. Cover dough with a sheet of greaseproof paper and weight down with baking beans. Return to refrigerator for ten minutes.

7 Bake pastry shell 'blind' for ten minutes. Then remove beans and paper, and continue to bake for ten to fifteen minutes longer, or until pastry is cooked through and lightly coloured.

8 Remove pastry from oven and leave to cool. Reduce oven temperature to moderate (375°F Mark 5).

9 Prepare cheese filling – an electric mixer will come in very useful if you have one. Squeeze out as much moisture from the cheese as possible: wrap it in a double thickness of muslin; twist the ends of the cloth as hard as you can, and squeeze the ball of cheese between your hands until the milky liquid stops oozing out of it.

10 Beat softened butter in electric mixer until light and fluffy. (Or use a wooden spoon.)

11 Have egg yolks, sifted icing sugar and curd cheese ready in three separate dishes. With the mixer turned to medium speed, add them alternately to the butter, a little at a time. Then continue to beat until smoothly blended, scraping sides of bowl towards the centre with a spatula to ensure that all of the mixture comes under the beaters.

12 Flavour cheese mixture sharply with lemon juice and grated rind, and add vanilla to taste, bearing in mind that flavours are weakened by cooking, and that this cheesecake should be rather lemony.

13 Sift flour over raisins or sultanas and candied peel. Toss fruit to coat them thoroughly and fold into cheese mixture.

14 Beat egg whites until stiff but not dry. Fold into cheese mixture with a large metal spoon or spatula.

5 Fill pastry case with cheese mixture, piling it up in the centre, as the cake tends to sink slightly in the middle when it cooks.

6 Bake cheesecake for fifty to fifty-five minutes until firm in the centre and well risen. If top of cake browns too quickly, cover it with greaseproof paper or crumpled foil.

7 When cake is cooked, remove from the oven and allow to cool in the tin before carefully unmoulding on to a serving dish.

8 To decorate: sift icing sugar over the top, or ice with a lemon water icing.

Paskha
(*Russian Easter cheesecake*)

Makes 12 generous portions

2–2¼lb curd cheese
6 egg yolks
10oz vanilla-flavoured castor sugar
½ pint double cream
½lb unsalted butter, softened
3–4oz blanched almonds, slivered
3 level tablespoons finely chopped candied peel
1 level tablespoon raisins
1 level tablespoon sultanas
1 level tablespoon finely chopped glacé cherries
1 level tablespoon finely chopped angelica
2–3 tablespoons lemon juice
Finely grated rind of 1 large lemon
Finely grated rind of 1 orange
¼–½ teaspoon vanilla essence

To decorate
Candied fruit, raisins, glacé cherries and angelica

A king among cheesecakes. *Paskha* is traditionally made just once a year, at Easter time, when Russians of the Orthodox faith break their strict Lenten fast with an incredibly rich bout of feasting.

The beautifully decorated dome of cheese shares pride of place with a feathery, brioche-like yeast cake called *kulich* which is also baked in a tall mould. The two are sliced and served together as a climax to the Easter feast.

As you will see, you have to start preparing a *paskha* at least two days before you wish to serve it. The cheese must first be squeezed dry of as much moisture as possible; then the *paskha* is left to drain and firm up under a heavy weight for at least twenty-four hours before unmoulding.

1 Use the large amount of cheese if it seems very moist. Wrap it up tightly in a double thickness of muslin. Place in a colander with a heavy weight on top and leave to drain overnight.

2 The following day, take the muslin-wrapped ball of cheese and twist the ends of the cloth firmly to squeeze out remaining liquid.

3 When cheese seems dry, unwrap it and put it in a large mixing bowl, or preferably in the bowl of an electric mixer.

4 Next, take a clean 6in flowerpot, an earthenware one if possible, as it absorbs moisture, and line it with a double thickness of muslin wrung out of cold water, cutting enough to fold over the top of the pot when it is full.

5 In the top of a double saucepan, wisk egg yolks with vanilla-flavoured castor sugar until thick and lemon-coloured. Gradually whisk in double cream until smoothly blended.

6 Set top of pan over simmering water and cook, stirring constantly, for ten to fifteen minutes, or until custard coats back of spoon thickly. Do not allow it to boil, or egg yolks will curdle. As soon as custard has thickened sufficiently, plunge base of pan into cold water to halt the cooking process.

7 Beat cheese vigorously with a large wooden spoon, or at medium speed in an electric mixer. When cheese is smooth, add softened butter a piece at a time, and continue to beat until smoothly blended. (If using an electric mixer, keep scraping sides of bowl

with a spatula to make sure all of the mixture comes under the beaters.)

Add hot custard, beating vigorously until mixture is well blended again.

If you have been using an electric mixer, switch it off at this stage and remove the bowl from the stand. Stir in remaining ingredients; then give the mixture a final beating to disperse them evenly throughout it.

Taste mixture and add more lemon juice or vanilla if necessary. It should be fragrant and rather sharply flavoured.

Pour cheese mixture into muslin-lined flowerpot and fold overlapping sides of muslin over the top to cover it completely.

If mixture is still rather liquid, as it will be if the custard was very hot when you blended it in, allow to cool. Then cover with a flat plate or saucer which just fits inside the rim of the flowerpot; weigh down heavily and leave in the refrigerator for at least twenty-four hours, standing on a dish to catch the syrupy liquid which will drain out of it.

To unmould *paskha*: fold back muslin and turn out on to a flat dish. Carefully peel off the muslin, which will have left an attractive pattern on the surface of the cheese.

To decorate *paskha*: stud the surface with small pieces of candied fruit, raisins, glacé cherries and angelica. Traditionally, the letters 'XB', which stand for the Easter salutation 'Christ is risen!' in the cyrillic alphabet, are incorporated into the decoration.

Any left over will keep for several days, covered, in the bottom of the refrigerator.

Lesson 8

Steamed and boiled puddings

British steamed puddings

The steamed pudding is a peculiarly British institution. A continental cook might raise an eyebrow and wonder at the menu that would tolerate such a hearty finale. And indeed, solid English puddings have acquired something of a reputation abroad. But, as with so many aspects of traditional British cooking, when a steamed pudding is good, it is very good indeed. And the traditional Christmas pudding, made to some treasured family recipe and carefully matured over many months, can be a positive triumph.

Steamed puddings suit the British winter – that uncomfortable blend of mildness and chilling damp, which penetrates clothing that would be adequate in a dry climate well below zero. They are substantial, but they need not be intolerably heavy. Even a Christmas pudding should have a light crumbly texture. And a steamed sponge pudding can be positively feathery.

The pudding batter

Basically, there are two types of batter suitable for steaming. One is a sponge-cake-type mixture in which butter is either creamed with the sugar, or rubbed into the flour. The other uses suet instead of fat. It's quite easy to see the difference: a steamed suet pudding has a much more crumbly, and in some ways lighter texture.

Commercially prepared shredded beef suet is a great convenience. If you want to prepare your own, make sure it is fresh, hard and dry. Remove any papery membrane or fibres before chopping it up into fine shreds with a long-bladed knife.

(Use some of the flour from your recipe to prevent the suet clogging up your knife blade.)

Fine *white breadcrumbs* may be substituted for part (usually half) of the flour to lighten the texture even more.

If you want a well-risen, airy pudding, aim for a rather soft batter. A Christmas-pudding-type affair, on the other hand, is quite stiff from the start, and hardly rises at all: it may swell up slightly in the centre, though, so to counteract this, hollow out a slight indentation in the middle with the back of your spoon.

Preparing the pudding basin

The pudding basin must be carefully buttered to make sure that the pudding comes out cleanly at the end. If butter refuses to adhere to the glazed surface, which it will do if there is the slightest suspicion of moisture there, or if the bowl is very cold, you will save a lot of time by using melted butter and applying it generously with a brush. When this sets, you can, if you wish, dust the surface with fine browned breadcrumbs, biscuit or macaroon crumbs, brown sugar or even chopped fruit and/or toasted nuts, shaking out the excess as you would from a cake tin.

Frequently the bottom of the basin is spread with jam, syrup or treacle which melts in the heat and, apart from its main aim of decorating the top of the pudding, makes it easier to turn it out. When no provision of this kind is made, you'd be safer to line the base with a circle of buttered greaseproof paper.

Having filled the basin, cover the surface of the pudding with another circle of buttered greaseproof paper.

Traditionally, the basin is sealed by tying on a cloth, but aluminium foil makes a far more effective and more convenient seal, tied tightly under the rim with a loop knot to make it easier to unravel.

If you still prefer to use a cloth, first rinse and wring it out of boiling water to make sure no trace of soap or detergent remains, then dust it lightly with flour. Tie on the cloth; bring the ends up over the top and pin them together neatly with a safety pin.

If the basin fits into the pan without much room to spare, fashion a string handle on top, or put the whole basin in one of those old-fashioned string shopping bags – not plastic or nylon, though – to enable you to lift it out again without scalding your fingers.

To steam a pudding

First find a saucepan large enough to take the pudding basin and cover tightly with a lid once it's in. A piece of wood or wad of newspaper in the bottom of the pan will prevent the pudding basin coming in too-direct contact with the heat.

Place the basin in the pan; pour in very hot water to come half or three-quarters of the way up the sides and bring to the boil.

Cover pan tightly; adjust heat so that water boils steadily and strongly without actually making the pudding basin rattle, and allow to boil for the required time. If you have to top up the pan, use boiling water; otherwise, you may crack the basin.

Alternatively, you can use a steamer. Again, it must be large enough to take the basin when the lid is firmly on, and care must be taken not to allow the pan underneath to boil dry.

To boil a pudding

A heavy suet pudding can also be boiled, literally, in a cloth.

First prepare the cloth as above, scalding it with boiling water and wringing it dry. Sprinkle lightly with flour and arrange in a round-bottomed bowl or colander, floured side up. Put in the pudding mixture; draw the sides of the cloth up over the top and tie together, leaving room for pudding to swell.

Immerse pudding completely in a pan of boiling water; bring to the boil again and boil steadily for the required time, topping up with more boiling water as necessary.

To turn out a pudding

Lift the basin out of the pan, steamer or whatever, and let it stand for a minute or two. Otherwise, the sudden outburst of steam might crack the surface of the pudding.

Remove cloth, foil and greaseproof paper, lay a heated serving dish on top of the basin and invert the two together. Shake gently once or twice until you feel the pudding come loose.

Carefully lift off basin, and peel off any greaseproof paper lining the bottom of the pudding.

If the pudding has been boiled in a cloth, let it drain thoroughly in a colander. Untie the string and gently pull the cloth away from the sides. Then invert pudding on to a serving dish and peel the cloth away completely.

To serve a pudding

The traditional English steamed or boiled pudding is rather dry, and fairly cries out for a sauce of some kind, a light custard or jam sauce, or hot syrup sharpened with lemon juice.

Nègre en chemise goes beautifully with chilled whipped cream, but this is rather lost on the more usual type of steamed pudding.

Always serve steamed puddings as hot as possible.

Basic steamed or boiled sponge pudding

Serves 6
8oz plain flour
2 level teaspoons baking powder
4oz butter
4oz castor sugar
2 eggs
About $\frac{1}{4}$ pint milk

Flavourings
Vanilla essence

Grated lemon rind
Mixed spice, cinnamon or ginger
2oz sultanas or raisins

To decorate basin
Butter
4–6 level tablespoons tart jam or warm syrup, honey or treacle

To serve
Fruit or custard sauce (*crème Anglaise* – see below)

1 Butter a 2 pint pudding basin and spread jam or syrup, etc., over the bottom and about a quarter of the way up sides.

2 Sift flour and baking powder into a bowl.

3 Rub in butter with your fingertips until mixture resembles fine breadcrumbs. Stir in sugar and make a well in the centre.

4 Beat eggs lightly. Pour them into the well, together with enough milk to make a batter with a good dropping consistency. Beat vigorously with a wooden spoon until batter is smoothly blended.

5 Beat in chosen flavouring.

6 Pour batter into prepared basin. Cover surface with a disc of buttered greaseproof paper; then cover basin tightly with a double thickness of foil, or tie on a pudding cloth.

7 Steam or boil pudding for one and a half to two hours until well risen and firm to the touch.

8 To serve: turn pudding out on to a hot serving dish and serve immediately with a custard or fruit sauce.

Crème Anglaise

Makes ½ pint
¾ pint milk
4 egg yolks

1–2oz castor sugar
1 level teaspoon cornflour (optional)
Flavouring (see method)

This light custard sauce makes a delicious alternative to whipped
cream for serving with ice cream, fruit-based desserts and other
creams or moulds. If you are worried about curdling the custard,
add the cornflour as a safeguard.

1 Pour milk into the top of double saucepan and bring to the boil
over direct heat.

2 Whisk egg yolks with sugar and cornflour, if used, until thick and
creamy. Add boiling milk gradually, beating vigorously.

3 Return mixture to top of double saucepan and cook over simmering
water, stirring constantly, until custard coats back of spoon. Take
great care not to let it reach boiling point or the egg yolks will
curdle. As soon as custard has thickened, plunge base of pan into
cold water to prevent further cooking.

4 Strain custard and stir in flavouring.

5 If custard is to be served hot, serve immediately, or keep hot by
placing pan in *warm* water. Otherwise, pour custard into a jug and
allow to cool, stirring occasionally to prevent a skin forming on
the surface; then cover jug and chill until ready to serve.

Flavourings A classic *crème Anglaise* is flavoured with vanilla, but
liqueur or strong coffee may also be used. For a chocolate *crème*,
melt about 2oz bitter chocolate in the milk before adding it to the
egg yolks, and use only 1oz sugar in the basic recipe.

Steamed apricot pudding

Serves 6
Butter
3oz castor sugar
4oz plain flour
2 eggs

12 canned apricot halves
Generous pinch of ground cinnamon
Finely grated rind of 1 orange
Juice of 1 lemon
2 level teaspoons baking powder
¾ pint apricot or custard sauce (*crème Anglaise* – see p.210),
   to serve

1 Grease a 3 pint pudding basin generously with butter.

2 Cream 3oz butter with the castor sugar until light and fluffy.

3 Sift flour; beat half of it into creamed mixture, together with 1 egg.

4 Beat vigorously until batter is well blended; then add remaining egg and flour, and beat again until smooth.

5 Pat apricot halves dry. Chop them up into ½in squares and fold them gently into the mixture, together with a generous pinch of cinnamon, the finely grated orange rind and lemon juice.

6 Finally, add baking powder and stir until well mixed.

7 Spoon batter into prepared basin. Cover surface with a disc of buttered greaseproof paper; then seal bowl with a double thickness of foil or by tying on a pudding cloth.

8 Boil or steam pudding for one and a half hours, or until well risen and firm to the touch.

9 To serve: turn pudding out on to a heated serving dish and serve hot with an apricot or custard sauce.

Brown bread and apple pudding

Serves 4–6
About 14 slices brown bread cut medium thick from a small
   loaf
About 4oz butter
1½lb cooking apples

Juice and finely grated rind of 1 large lemon
3oz Demerara sugar
2 level tablespoons raisins
Generous pinch of ground cloves
$\frac{1}{4}$ level teaspoon ground cinnamon
$\frac{3}{4}$ pint rich custard sauce (*crème Anglaise* – see p.210), to serve

1 Trim bread of crusts and butter each slice generously.

2 Butter a 2 pint pudding basin generously and line base and sides completely with some of the bread slices, buttered sides inwards.

3 Peel, core and cut apples into small chunks. Toss them thoroughly with lemon juice and finely grated lemon rind, the sugar, raisins and spices. (If using dessert apples, cut sugar by 1oz.)

4 Pack half the apple mixture into the bread-lined basin and dot with a level tablespoon of butter in flakes.

5 Cover surface with more bread slices, buttered side up, and fill to the top with remaining apple mixture. Press down lightly; dot with another tablespoon of butter and cover surface entirely with remaining bread slices, buttered side down this time.

6 Cover basin tightly with a sheet of buttered greaseproof paper and then with a piece of foil.

7 Steam pudding for one and a half hours.

8 Remove foil and greaseproof paper. Turn pudding out carefully and serve hot with a custard sauce (or cream).

Canary pudding

Serves 6
Butter
3 standard eggs plus their weight in softened butter, castor sugar and plain flour (about 6oz of each)
Pinch of salt
Finely grated rind of 1 lemon

½ level teaspoon baking powder
¾ pint *crème Anglaise* (see p.210) flavoured with a little lemon
  rind and juice

1 Butter a 2 pint pudding basin generously.

2 Sift flour with a pinch of salt.

3 In a bowl, beat softened butter with a wooden spoon until creamy.

4 Add sugar and grated lemon rind, and beat until light and fluffy.

5 Beat in 1 egg; then add half the sifted flour and blend thoroughly.

6 Add remaining eggs one at a time alternately with remaining flour,
   beating vigorously to make a smooth batter.

7 Finally, sift in baking powder and blend thoroughly.

8 Turn mixture into prepared pudding basin, making a slight hollow
   in the centre with the back of your spoon so that pudding will rise
   evenly. Cover with a buttered paper.

9 Tie on a cloth with string or seal top of bowl tightly with a double
   thickness of foil to ensure that no water can seep in.

10 Steam or boil pudding for one and a half hours.

11 To serve: turn pudding out on to a serving dish. Mask with some
    of the *crème Anglaise* and serve remainder in a sauceboat.

Castle puddings

Serves 6
Butter
3 standard eggs plus their weight in softened butter, castor
  sugar and plain flour (about 6oz of each)
Pinch of salt
Finely grated rind of 1 lemon

½ level teaspoon baking powder
¾ pint *crème Anglaise* (p.210) flavoured with a little lemon rind
   and juice (or melted jam sauce sharpened with lemon juice),
   to serve

To decorate moulds
Butter
Pieces of glacé cherry

1 Butter six ¼ pint dariole or turret moulds and decorate with a
few small pieces of glacé cherry.

2 Prepare mixture as for *canary pudding*, Steps 2–7 (p.214).

3 Half-fill moulds with pudding mixture. Cover surface of each
pudding with a disc of lightly buttered greaseproof paper and seal
moulds with foil.

4 Arrange moulds in a pan with boiling water to come a third of the
way up sides and simmer, covered, for forty minutes.

5 Turn out and serve with *crème Anglaise* or melted jam sauce
sharpened with lemon juice.

Chelsea treacle pudding

Serves 6
1–2 level tablespoons butter
4oz shredded beef suet
4oz fresh white breadcrumbs
4oz plain flour
1 level teaspoon baking powder
Pinch of salt
4oz currants
4oz raisins
¼ pint treacle
½ pint milk
Custard sauce (*crème Anglaise* – see p.210), to serve

Grease a 2 pint pudding basin with butter.

2 In a large bowl, combine beef suet with breadcrumbs. Sift in flour together with baking powder and a pinch of salt, and mix well.

3 Wash dried fruit if necessary and squeeze out as much moisture as possible in a clean cloth. Add to the bowl; stir until well mixed and make a hollow in the centre.

4 Warm treacle gently in a heavy pan. Stir in milk. Then pour liquid into the hollow of the mixture, beating vigorously with a wooden spoon to make a smooth batter.

5 Pour batter into prepared basin. Cover surface with a disc of buttered greaseproof paper; then cover bowl tightly with a double thickness of foil, or tie on a pudding cloth.

6 Boil or steam pudding for three hours, topping up with more water as necessary to prevent it boiling dry.

7 To serve pudding: turn out on to a heated serving dish and mask with a rich custard sauce. Serve more sauce separately in a sauceboat.

Nègre en chemise

Serves 6
4oz trimmed white bread
½ pint double cream
Softened butter
4 eggs
2 egg yolks
1oz ground almonds
Castor sugar
4oz bitter chocolate, melted

1 Soak bread in ¼ pint cream for five minutes.

2 In a large bowl beat 2oz softened butter until fluffy. Work in soaked bread until completely blended. Add eggs, egg yolks, ground almonds and 1oz sugar, beating vigorously between each addition. (Mixture may curdle when eggs are added, but this does not matter as chocolate will bind it again.)

3 Add half of egg mixture to melted chocolate and beat well; then combine with remaining egg mixture and continue to beat vigorously until thoroughly blended.

4 Butter a tall, tapering, 1½ pint mould – a metal measuring jug will do – and line base with a circle of buttered greaseproof paper. Pour in chocolate mixture and make a slight hollow in the centre with the back of your spoon. Cover top of mould tightly with foil or a pudding cloth.

5 Place mould in a pan with water to come halfway up sides. Bring to the boil; cover pan and steam for one and a half hours, topping up water in the pan as necessary.

6 To serve: whip remaining cream and sweeten lightly with castor sugar.

7 Turn mould out; pipe generous swirls of cream around base and serve immediately before cream melts from heat of pudding.

Old English Christmas pudding

Makes 2 puddings
12oz sultanas
12oz raisins
12oz currants
12oz shredded suet
8oz fresh white breadcrumbs
8oz soft dark brown sugar
4oz self-raising flour, sifted
4oz chopped mixed peel
2oz grated raw carrot
1 level teaspoon mixed spice
½ level teaspoon freshly grated nutmeg
¼ level teaspoon salt
2 level tablespoons treacle or golden syrup
½ level teaspoon finely grated orange rind
½ level teaspoon finely grated lemon rind
4 tablespoons fresh orange juice
2 tablespoons lemon juice

4 large eggs, lightly beaten
$\frac{1}{4}$ pint barley wine (or stout)
6–8 tablespoons brandy

For pudding basins
Butter
Greaseproof paper
Pudding cloths and string

To serve
A sprig of holly
Sifted icing sugar
Brandy
Brandy sauce (p.219) *or*
Brandy butter (p.220)

As you will see, a home-made Christmas pudding is no last-minute whim. First the raw mixture has to stand overnight before cooking, and then the pudding must be left to mature in a cool, dry place for a minimum of four months, preferably longer. Those who insist that a Christmas pudding should be allowed to mature for a year manage to do this by preparing during one Christmas season the pudding they intend to serve at the next, thus keeping one step ahead of themselves all the time, a degree of dedication I have never quite achieved.

1 Pick over dried fruit; wash and dry thoroughly on a cloth only if necessary.

2 In a large porcelain or earthenware bowl, assemble first twelve ingredients and toss together until thoroughly mixed. Make a large well in the centre.

3 In another, smaller bowl, blend treacle or syrup thoroughly with grated orange and lemon rinds. Blend in orange and lemon juice gradually, and when mixture is smooth again, beat in lightly beaten eggs, barley wine and brandy.

4 Pour this mixture into dried ingredients and stir vigorously with a large wooden spoon until well blended. (Don't forget to make a wish with the last three stirs!)

5 Cover bowl with a damp cloth and leave overnight in a cool place to allow flavours to develop.

6 The following day, start by preparing your pudding basins. Grease two 2½ pint basins with butter and line bottoms with circles of buttered greaseproof paper.

7 Divide pudding mixture evenly between prepared basins, levelling off tops.

8 Cover top of each pudding with another circle of buttered greaseproof paper; then cover basins with pudding cloths and tie down with string.

9 Steam puddings for three hours, taking care not to let water underneath dry out. Allow to cool before storing in a cool, dry cupboard.

10 On the day you wish to serve a pudding, steam it slowly for two hours until thoroughly reheated.

11 To serve: turn pudding out on to a heated serving dish. Decorate with holly (if it's Christmas time) and a sifting of icing sugar, and flame with brandy at the table. (To avoid an anticlimax it is best to heat the brandy in a large metal ladle or spoon and set it alight *before* pouring it over the pudding.) Serve with brandy sauce, brandy butter or whatever accompaniment is traditional in your family.

This recipe makes two puddings, each serving eight. In some families the second pudding is saved up for Easter, by which time its flavour has reached a peak of perfection.

Brandy sauce (for Christmas pudding)

Makes ½ pint
4 egg yolks
4 level tablespoons double cream
4 tablespoons brandy
2 level tablespoons castor sugar

1 Combine ingredients in the top of a double saucepan. Add 4 tablespoons water.

2 Set pan over lightly simmering water and whisk for six to eight minutes to make a thick, frothy sauce. Do not allow sauce to boil, as it will curdle.

3 Serve warm or cold.

Brandy butter (for Christmas pudding)

Makes ½lb
4oz butter
4oz castor sugar
2 tablespoons brandy

1 Soften butter with a wooden spoon; then beat until smooth and fluffy.

2 Put aside 1 level tablespoon castor sugar. Add remainder to creamed butter gradually, beating vigorously until mixture is very fluffy and almost white.

3 Soak remaining sugar in brandy. Incorporate into butter cream a little at a time, and beat until smooth again. Chill until firm.

Lesson 9

Moulded desserts

Although we no longer go in for great towering edifices of moulded desserts like those that grace the colour plates of Victorian cookery books – the tension when turning these out must have been quite unbearable – a pretty moulded cream, set just firmly enough to hold its shape without rubberising the texture, is a satisfying thing to make.

The simplest example of a moulded dessert is a jelly. Then come the Bavarian creams and cold soufflés, which are two variations on the same theme of whisked egg yolks, cream and stiffly beaten egg whites, helped to set with gelatine.

Indeed, with the exception of the clear jellies, you should never regard gelatine as the major setting agent in moulded sweets, but rather as an aid to the cooked eggs and whipped cream which should do most of the work themselves.

How to use gelatine

Handling gelatine no longer presents the problems that it once did, what with clumsy, thick brown sheets that often burned before they would melt, had a nasty flavour reminiscent of carpenter's glue, and varied considerably and quite unpredictably in strength from brand to brand. Nowadays, powdered gelatine of high quality is packed in clearly labelled sachets which state the weight, or, in some cases, the setting power. You should always look out for this, especially when using a brand that is new to you. If, for example, your recipe calls for ½oz and the contents of the sachet are said to be *the equivalent of ½oz*, be guided by the manufacturer, even though the contents may not actually *weigh* ½oz exactly. (Our recipes all give gelatine in fractions of an ounce, except for very small quantities of less than a tablespoon, to allow for any adjustment you may need to make.)

Leaf gelatine, which used to be the usual form in which it was sold, has now largely been superseded by the powdered variety. If you prefer to use leaf gelatine, weigh out the exact equivalent of ½oz and make a note of the number of leaves for future reference – usually it works out to about six fine leaves to the ounce.

Gelatine should never be added to a mixture in its dry state. The usual procedure, which applies to both leaf and powder, is first to soak it thoroughly, then to heat the soaked mixture gently until completely dissolved.

To dissolve powdered gelatine Sprinkle granules over cold liquid in a small bowl or cup (water, or a little of the recipe liquid, according to the recipe method), and leave to soak for several minutes. The gelatine will absorb the liquid and, if only a little liquid has been used, be quite solid again. Now place the cup in hot water, and when gelatine starts to melt around the sides, stir gently until liquid is quite, quite clear.

For some dishes, especially those in which the gelatine is combined with a hot mixture, the second stage can be omitted. The gelatine is simply softened in a larger amount of liquid, and beaten into hot liquid. Remember, though, that gelatine should not be boiled, so all the cooking must be finished and the pan removed from the heat *before* it is added.

Working with gelatine Dissolved gelatine is usually added to a mixture when it is *just* lukewarm. For best results, the liquid gelatine and the mixture should be at the same temperature. If the mixture is too cold, you run the risk of the gelatine setting into nasty little lumps or 'ropes' before you have had time to blend it in.

Having thoroughly incorporated the gelatine, the mixture is usually left to cool until it is *just on the point* of setting, i.e. it must not be stiff enough to hold a clean edge, otherwise you will not be able to fold anything else in smoothly. On the other hand, if it is too liquid, anything airy that you attempt to incorporate, such as beaten egg white, will have all its volume and lightness crushed out of it.

When time is short and you want to speed up the cooling process of a gelatine mixture, stand the bowl in a few inches of cold water and leave to cool, occasionally drawing a large metal spoon around the sides and through the centre to prevent the mixture setting firmly around the sides and on the base, where it is in contact with the cold bowl.

On the other hand, should you find that the mixture has set suddenly when your back was turned, just replace the bowl over a pan of hot water for half a minute or so and let it soften again, folding and drawing it away from the sides of the bowl with your spoon to keep the texture even.

Folding ingredients into a gelatine mixture

Cream Many dishes have whipped cream folded into the gelatine mixture towards the end. The important thing to remember here is that the consistency of the cream should be more or less the same as that of the mixture into which it is being incorporated. This means that the cream must be whisked with great care, preferably by hand, since it is only too easy to overbeat it, and if it is too stiff you are likely to end up with pockets of unblended cream in your mixture. Some recipes advise adding a tablespoon or two of very cold milk to the cream before beating it. This makes it easier to control by slowing down the rate at which it thickens.

Egg whites Stop whisking as soon as they stand up in firm, soft peaks when the beaters are lifted. Do not let them go 'dry'.

In either case, if you have overbeaten by mistake and feel that the cream or egg whites will not fold in easily, reverse the process and start by folding some of the cool gelatine mixture into the cream (or egg whites). Then, having loosened the latter, carefully fold it all back into the gelatine mixture.

To turn out a jelly or moulded sweet

The moment of truth that causes so much unnecessary heartbreak. I have found no justification for rinsing the mould out with cold water as so many cookbooks advise. Provided the mould is clean and the contents quite set, you should have no trouble in turning it out.

* Fill a basin with very hot water.

* Select the dish on which you intend to serve the jelly or mould. It should be large and flat for the mould to stand steady. Wet the plate lightly so that if the mould does not land on it dead centre you will be able to coax it into position.

* Draw the tip of a knife around the outer rim of the mould. Then immerse the mould in hot water for *one or two seconds only* – no longer. Far better to repeat the dipping if the mould refuses to come out than to risk melting the surface away.

* Lay the plate in position on top of the mould and, holding the plate and mould together with both hands, quickly reverse them. Halfway over, give them a quick jerk to loosen the side so that if the mould is being held fast by an airlock, this will be released. Turn the mould right over on to the dish. Give one or two firm shakes – you will feel the weight of the jelly or pudding transfer itself to the plate.

* When you are sure it has come loose, lay the plate down and slowly, with both hands, slip the mould off.

* Wipe the sides of the dish clean.

* If the outer surface of the pudding has melted slightly, slip it into the refrigerator to firm up again.

* Metal moulds need a very short immersion in water as they conduct heat so efficiently. In fact, it is often enough to wrap a cloth wrung out of very hot water around them for a second or two to loosen

the contents. Porcelain and earthenware moulds are trickier, and may require more than one dipping before the pudding comes loose.

To serve moulded desserts

There is one golden rule – never serve a moulded dessert that has been set with gelatine straight from the refrigerator, especially if it has been left there to chill overnight. Aim to allow it about an hour at room temperature to take the chill off and restore softness to the texture.

And if the mould has been damaged on its way out, remember that a piping-bagful of whipped cream, judiciously used, will camouflage all but the most disastrous mishap.

Cold soufflés

The cold soufflé (*soufflé froid*) is not really a soufflé at all, but a concoction of whipped eggs, sugar and cream, flavoured with fruit, chocolate, or whatever, and made light and delicate with stiffly beaten egg whites.

The texture of the soufflé is all important, and for this reason great care must be taken when adding gelatine. Too little, and it will not hold its shape – too much and it will be just like trying to eat your way through foam rubber.

The illusion of a soufflé is created by extending the height of the soufflé dish with a firm collar, enabling you to take the mixture about a third again above the rim. The soufflé is then left to set and, just before serving, the paper collar is peeled off to reveal what to all appearances is a genuine soufflé with a beautifully risen 'head'.

To shape a 'collar' for a cold soufflé

The best way of shaping a collar is to cut a band of greaseproof paper about 10in wide, and long enough to go round the soufflé dish with an overlap of about 1½in. Fold it in half lengthwise, i.e. to make a long band 5in wide.

Wrap the band round the dish and, with a pencil, mark the spot where the two ends meet. Then remove dish and pin the two ends of the band together at the base corner, making the collar slightly tighter than indicated by your pencil mark.

Now comes the test: carefully drop the dish down into the collar and pull the latter up around it to come about 3in above the rim of the dish. *The fit should be tight enough to allow you to lift the dish by its collar without any fear of it slipping off.*

Pin the top of the collar in position. Finally, stand the prepared soufflé dish on a plate, so that you will be able to transport it back and forth without damaging the collar.

I realise that many people simply tie the collar on as tightly as possible with string. If this method works for you, well and good. However, I think you will find the procedure outlined above worth the little extra time it takes in that it guarantees a neat, safe result.

To remove collar

Just before serving, and having made sure the soufflé is quite set, unpin the collar. Take a knife with a long blade and hold it upright, handle upwards, against the side of the soufflé, close to the end where you intend to start pulling the paper away. Then, with your other hand, take hold of the paper collar and carefully peel it away against the back of the knife. In this way you will avoid pulling large chunks of soufflé off with the paper.

The exposed sides of the soufflé can either be left bare to show off its texture, or decorated by pressing on chopped nuts or coarsely grated chocolate. Finish with piped whipped cream and fruit or chocolate curls on top.

Cold chocolate soufflé

Serves 6–8
1 medium-sized orange
1 level tablespoon instant coffee
5oz bitter chocolate
½oz powdered gelatine

6 eggs
4oz castor sugar
$\frac{1}{2}$ pint double cream
1–2 tablespoons brandy, rum or liqueur (optional)
Coarsely grated bitter chocolate and whipped cream, to
    decorate

Fit a standing collar of greaseproof paper around a 7in soufflé dish (measured across the top), to come 3in above the rim (see p.225).

Select two bowls, a large one for beating the eggs and a smaller one for melting chocolate. Find a saucepan over which both bowls will fit securely. Pour in water. Fit each bowl in position over the pan and check that base does not touch water. Put water on to heat gently.

Scrub the orange clean and dry it thoroughly with a cloth. Finely grate rind into the smaller bowl. Squeeze juice and strain it into the same bowl. Add instant coffee, dissolved in 3 tablespoons boiling water, and chocolate, broken into small pieces. Put aside.

In a small bowl or cup, sprinkle gelatine over 4 tablespoons cold water and put aside to soften until needed.

Break eggs into the large bowl. Add sugar.

When water in saucepan comes to the boil, reduce heat to a bare simmer. Fit bowl containing eggs and sugar over pan, and whisk vigorously until mixture is light and bulky, and leaves a trail on the surface when beaters are lifted.

Remove bowl and in its place put the smaller bowl containing chocolate mixture. Heat gently until chocolate has completely melted.

Meanwhile, continue to whisk egg mixture until barely lukewarm.

When chocolate has melted, remove from heat. Remove saucepan of water from heat as well. Stand bowl (or cup) containing softened gelatine in the hot water and stir until completely dissolved. Remove.

10 Whisk chocolate mixture lightly to ensure it is quite free of lumps.

11 When chocolate mixture and dissolved gelatine are both just warm, blend them together thoroughly.

12 Pour cream into a bowl and whisk carefully until it is just thick enough to leave a barely perceptible trail on the surface. (If you have been using an electric mixer so far, this operation may be safer done with a hand whisk to avoid overbeating cream.)

13 Quickly and lightly fold chocolate gelatine mixture into cream. Then, before mixture has had a chance to start setting, fold it into the cooled whisked egg mixture, together with brandy, rum or liqueur, if used. Stop folding as soon as you have got rid of chocolate 'streaks' in mixture.

14 Stand prepared soufflé dish on a plate. Pour in soufflé mixture, taking care not to dislodge or crumple paper collar. Leave it to firm slightly for fifteen to twenty minutes before transferring dish to the refrigerator.

15 Chill soufflé for two to three hours until firmly set.

16 Just before serving: peel off paper collar (see p.226). Press coarsely grated bitter chocolate around exposed sides of soufflé and decorate top with grated chocolate and piped whipped cream.

Cold lemon soufflé

Serves 4–5

4 eggs
½oz powdered gelatine
7oz castor sugar
Finely grated rind and strained juice of 4 large lemons
½ pint double cream
Whipped cream and chopped toasted nuts, to decorate
    (optional)

1 Fit a standing collar of greaseproof paper around a 5¾in soufflé dish (measured across the top), to come at least 3in above the rim (see p.225).

Select two bowls, one larger than the other, and a saucepan over which the larger bowl will fit securely. Pour 2in or 3in water into pan and put it on to heat. Make quite sure that the smaller bowl is perfectly clean and dry.

Separate eggs, dropping yolks into larger bowl and whites into smaller one.

Sprinkle gelatine over 4 tablespoons cold water in a cup and leave to soften.

Add sugar to egg yolks. Fit bowl over pan of water, which should be barely simmering, and whisk vigorously until mixture is thick and light, and leaves a trail on the surface when beaters are lifted.

Gradually whisk in lemon juice and continue to whisk until mixture thickens again. This time it will just manage to hold a trail on the surface. Remove pan from heat and lift off bowl.

Place cup containing softened gelatine in the hot water to dissolve, stirring occasionally.

Meanwhile, continue to whisk egg yolk mixture until just lukewarm.

When gelatine has completely dissolved, remove cup from water. Allow to cool slightly. Whisk into egg yolk mixture. Fold in finely grated lemon rind.

Whisk cream until a trail just holds its shape on the surface, being careful not to let it go too far, or it will be difficult to fold in. The texture should be about the same as that of the egg mixture.

Make sure your whisk is perfectly clean and dry. Whisk egg whites until they hold their shape in floppy peaks.

With a large metal spoon or spatula, fold cream into egg mixture, followed by beaten egg whites, working as lightly and quickly as possible.

13 Stand prepared soufflé dish on a plate. Pour in soufflé mixture, taking care not to dislodge or crumple paper collar. Leave it to firm slightly for fifteen to twenty minutes before transferring dish to the refrigerator.

14 Chill soufflé for two to three hours until firmly set.

15 Just before serving: peel off paper collar (see p.226). If liked, decorate top of soufflé with swirls of piped whipped cream and press chopped toasted nuts around exposed sides.

Cold orange soufflé

Serves 6–8
5 medium-sized oranges
1 lemon
$\frac{3}{4}$oz powdered gelatine
6 eggs
8oz castor sugar
$\frac{1}{2}$ pint double cream
2–3 tablespoons Grand Marnier (optional)
Whipped cream and fresh orange segments, to decorate

1 Fit a standing collar of greaseproof paper around a 7in soufflé dish (measured across the top), to come 3in above the rim (see p.225).

2 Select a large bowl and a saucepan over which it will fit comfortably. Fill saucepan with water to a depth of about 2in; bring water to simmering point.

3 Scrub oranges and lemon. Finely grate rinds of 2 oranges and 1 lemon into bowl. Squeeze juice of all the oranges and the lemon, and strain into bowl.

4 Pour off 3 tablespoons strained juice into a small bowl or cup. Sprinkle gelatine over it and leave to soften.

5 Separate eggs, dropping yolks into bowl with fruit juice, and whites into another bowl that is quite clean and dry.

Add sugar to bowl containing egg yolks and juice. Fit bowl over pan of simmering water and beat with a whisk until mixture is very fluffy and pale, and leaves a trail on the surface when beaters are lifted.

Remove bowl and pan from heat. Place bowl on the table. Stand cup or bowl containing softened gelatine in the remaining hot water and let it dissolve completely, stirring occasionally.

Meanwhile, continue to whisk orange egg mixture until cool.

Add dissolved gelatine and continue to whisk until thoroughly blended. Leave until completely cold and on the point of setting.

Whisk egg whites until stiff but not dry.

Whisk cream until floppy and of the same consistency as the cold orange mixture.

With a large metal spoon or spatula, fold cream into orange mixture, followed by stiffly beaten egg whites and liqueur, if used.

Stand prepared soufflé dish on a plate. Pour in soufflé mixture, taking care not to dislodge or crumple paper collar. Leave it to firm up slightly for fifteen to twenty minutes before transferring dish to the refrigerator.

Chill soufflé for at least two hours until firmly set.

Just before serving: peel off paper collar (see p.226) and decorate soufflé with piped whipped cream and sections of fresh orange.

Mousse glacée au chocolat

Serves 6–8
4 level teaspoons powdered gelatine
8oz bitter chocolate
2 egg yolks
4½oz icing sugar
17 fluid oz milk

1 level tablespoon powdered coffee
1 pint double cream
Vanilla essence
Coarsely grated chocolate, to decorate

1 Sprinkle gelatine over 2 tablespoons cold water in a cup and put aside to soften.

2 Break chocolate into the top of a double saucepan and allow to melt over simmering water, stirring occasionally with a wooden spoon.

3 Put egg yolks in a large bowl; sift in icing sugar and beat until smooth and fluffy.

4 Dissolve gelatine by standing cup in a bowl of hot water and stirring until liquid is quite clear.

5 When chocolate has melted, bring milk to the boil. Add to chocolate gradually, beating well with a wooden spoon to avoid small lumps forming. Beat in powdered coffee, followed by dissolved gelatine.

6 Pour hot chocolate milk over egg yolk mixture in a thin stream, beating vigorously with a wire whisk. Allow to cool.

7 When mixture is on the point of setting, beat cream with a whisk until it stands in soft peaks. Fold gently but thoroughly into chocolate mixture, using a metal spoon. Flavour with a few drops of vanilla essence.

8 Pour chocolate mixture into a 2 pint mould and leave to set in the refrigerator, preferably overnight.

9 To serve: turn out mould on to a flat serving dish (see p.224). Decorate with coarsely grated chocolate and serve.

Apple apricot mousse

Serves 6
½lb dried apricots (see note), soaked overnight
1lb cooking apples

Finely grated rind and juice of ½ lemon
1½oz powdered gelatine
2 eggs, separated
3oz sugar, or to taste
¼ pint double cream
1 teaspoon vanilla essence
1–2 drops almond essence
1–2 drops orange food colouring (optional)
Whipped cream and toasted almond slivers, to decorate

If you have an electric blender, you can make a smoother purée of the fruit than obtainable with a sieve but, of course, the apples must then be cored and peeled before they are cooked.

The type of dried apricots used makes a difference to the final result: try to find the soft, plump variety which are paler in colour and less tart than the small, hard, bright-orange kind.

The mousse can also be made with dried peaches.

Drain soaked apricots and measure off ¼ pint soaking liquid into a medium-sized pan. Add apricots.

If intending to use an electric blender to purée fruit (see note above), peel and core apples. Otherwise simply wipe them with a damp cloth. Chop apples coarsely and combine with apricots. Add finely grated rind and juice of ½ lemon.

Place pan over a moderate heat. Bring to the boil; cover and simmer gently for about twenty minutes, or until apricots are very soft and apples disintegrating.

Meanwhile, sprinkle gelatine over 5 tablespoons cold water in a small bowl or cup and leave to soften for about five minutes. Then stand bowl (or cup) in hot water and stir until gelatine has dissolved and liquid is quite clear. Cool slightly.

Beat egg yolks lightly with a fork.

When fruits are cooked, rub them through a fine sieve or purée in an electric blender, together with all their juices.

7 Blend egg yolks into hot fruit purée and sweeten to taste with sugar.

8 Pour fruit purée into a 2 pint measuring jug. When purée is just lukewarm, beat in dissolved gelatine.

9 Measure purée and, if necessary, stir in a little cold water to make it up to 1½ pints. Pour into a large bowl and allow to cool until just on the point of setting.

10 Whisk cream until just stiff enough to leave a faint trail on the surface when beaters are lifted. It should be of about the same consistency as the fruit purée.

11 Make sure your whisk is perfectly clean and dry. Whisk egg whites until they hold their shape in floppy peaks.

12 With a large metal spoon or spatula, fold cream into fruit purée, followed by beaten egg whites.

13 Flavour mousse to taste with vanilla and just a drop or two of almond essence. If the apricots have not coloured mousse sufficiently, you can liven it up with a drop or two of orange (or mixed red and yellow) food colouring.

14 Pour mousse into a 2½ pint mould. Chill until set.

15 To serve: turn mould out on to a dish (see p.224). Decorate with blobs of whipped cream and spike with toasted almond slivers.

Coffee cream bavarois

Serves 6–8
1½oz bitter chocolate
¾ pint milk
6 egg yolks
6oz castor sugar
2 level tablespoons instant coffee
2 tablespoons orange liqueur
½oz powdered gelatine
4 tablespoons very cold milk

½ pint double cream
Flavourless cooking oil, for mould

To decorate
2 level tablespoons freshly roasted coffee beans
1 tablespoon orange liqueur
Whipped cream

Use a good-quality dark chocolate for a really rich, smooth flavour.

1 Break chocolate into small pieces. In the top of a double saucepan, scald milk over direct heat. Add chocolate and stir until dissolved.

2 Beat egg yolks with sugar until fluffy and lemon-coloured. Add scalded milk mixture gradually, beating constantly.

3 Dissolve instant coffee in 3 tablespoons boiling water. Stir into milk mixture. Pour back into top of double saucepan and cook over lightly simmering water, stirring constantly, until mixture coats back of spoon, about twenty minutes. Take care not to let it boil, or egg yolks will curdle.

4 As soon as custard has thickened, plunge pan into cold water to arrest cooking process and cool custard slightly. Stir in liqueur.

5 Soften gelatine in 3 tablespoons cold water. Then put basin in a pan of hot water (the bottom half of the double saucepan is the most convenient), and stir until gelatine has completely dissolved and liquid is clear. Stir into cooling custard. Leave until cold and just on the point of setting.

6 Add cold milk to double cream and whisk until floppy. Ideally, it should have the same consistency as the cold custard, so that the two can be combined with the minimum of folding. Fold cream into cold custard.

7 Brush a 2 pint mould with flavourless oil. Pour in *bavarois* mixture and chill until set, two hours at least.

8 To unmould *bavarois*: dip mould in hot water *for two to three seconds only* to loosen cream – not too long, or cream will begin to melt. Turn out carefully on to a serving dish, and return to the bottom of the refrigerator until an hour before serving.

9 To decorate *bavarois*: macerate coffee beans in orange liqueur for at least thirty minutes, longer if possible. Drain them and chop them coarsely with a knife.

10 Just before serving: decorate *bavarois* with whipped cream and sprinkle with chopped coffee beans.

Hazelnut bavarois

Serves 6–8

7oz hazelnuts
¼ pint milk
4oz castor sugar
Pinch of salt
4 egg yolks
1 tablespoon lemon juice
1 teaspoon vanilla essence
Flavourless cooking oil, for mould
½oz powdered gelatine
1 pint double cream
2–3 level tablespoons crushed praline (see note)

A *bavarois* need not necessarily be made with chocolate, coffee or fruit. Here is a deliciously rich one flavoured with hazelnuts and praline.

Failing home-made praline, use bought almond (or even peanut) brittle, crushed with a rolling pin or pounded in a mortar.

1 Grill hazelnuts under a hot grill, shaking the pan frequently to prevent them burning, until skins become dry and brittle. Rub skins off by rolling hazelnuts between the palms of your hands (or between two sheets of greaseproof paper). Grind 6oz hazelnuts in a *mouli*. Chop remainder coarsely or leave them whole.

2 In the top of a double saucepan, stir milk with sugar and salt over direct heat until sugar has melted.

3 Beat egg yolks in a bowl. Blend in a little of the hot milk mixture, then pour back into the pan and continue to cook over hot water until custard thickens, stirring frequently. Do not allow custard to boil, or egg yolks will curdle.

4 Remove pan from heat and plunge base into cold water to halt cooking process. Cool slightly; add lemon juice and vanilla essence, to taste, and leave to become quite cold, stirring occasionally to prevent a skin forming on the surface.

5 Brush a 2 pint, straight-sided mould with flavourless oil.

6 Sprinkle gelatine over 2 tablespoons cold water in a cup, and leave for five minutes until softened. Then stand cup in a bowl of hot water and stir until gelatine has dissolved and liquid is quite clear. Blend dissolved gelatine with cooling custard, and leave until on the point of setting.

7 Whip cream until floppy. Fold into custard, together with all the hazelnuts and praline.

8 Pour into prepared mould and chill in the refrigerator until firmly set.

9 To unmould: dip mould in hot water for just ten seconds to loosen it, and turn out carefully on to a flat serving dish (see p.224). The *bavarois* may be decorated with hazelnuts dipped in caramel or a sprinkling of more finely pounded praline.

To make praline In a small, heavy pan, melt 4oz granulated sugar with 4 tablespoons water and 1 teaspoon lemon juice. Bring to the boil and boil until syrup turns into a rich, golden caramel (340°F on a sugar thermometer). Add 4oz almonds, blanched and toasted to a deep golden colour. Mix well. Pour on to a marble slab, or some other cold surface which you have brushed with oil, and leave until cold and hard. Use as required.

Raspberry bavarois

Serves 6
1lb frozen raspberries
3oz castor sugar
3 egg yolks
½ pint milk
½oz powdered gelatine
Juice of 1 lemon
½ pint double cream
Butter, for mould

1 Place frozen raspberries in a sieve over a bowl and sprinkle with 1oz of the castor sugar. Leave until completely defrosted.

2 Whisk remaining sugar with egg yolks until light and fluffy.

3 Scald milk. Pour over egg and sugar mixture gradually, beating constantly.

4 Transfer mixture to the top of a double saucepan and stir over simmering water until sauce thickens enough to coat the back of a wooden spoon. Take care not to let it boil, or egg yolks will curdle. Remove from heat and cool slightly.

5 Meanwhile, soften gelatine for five minutes in 4 tablespoons of the syrup drained from the raspberries; then stir over hot water until liquid is clear and gelatine completely dissolved.

6 Cool gelatine mixture slightly. Blend with cooling custard.

7 Crush two-thirds of the raspberries, reserving the best ones, and press them through a sieve to make a purée. Blend purée with custard; then fold in whole fruit, taking care not to crush them. Add lemon juice, to taste.

8 Whip half the cream lightly. Fold into raspberry custard.

9 Brush a 2 pint decorative mould with about 1 tablespoon melted butter. Pour in the raspberry cream and chill in the refrigerator until firm.

0 When ready to serve: whip remaining cream stiffly.

1 Dip mould for one or two seconds only into very hot water. Turn *bavarois* out on to a serving dish and pipe whipped cream in a decorative pattern over top and sides. Serve very cold.

Semolina cream mould with blackcurrant sauce

Serves 4–6
1lb fresh or frozen blackcurrants
4oz icing sugar, sifted
1 pint milk
3oz semolina
2 eggs, separated
3oz castor sugar
4 level tablespoons double cream
1 teaspoon vanilla essence
1 tablespoon lemon juice
1 level tablespoon softened butter

Do not be dismayed at the thought of a semolina pudding. Nothing could be less like the hated memories of your childhood than this elegant French sweet.

1 Remove stalks from fresh blackcurrants. Rinse them quickly in a sieve or colander under the cold tap; drain well, shaking off as much moisture as possible. If using frozen currants, defrost them according to instructions on packet.

2 Rub blackcurrants through a fine sieve; or blend them in an electric liquidiser, then rub purée through the sieve. Beat in sifted icing sugar.

3 Bring milk to the boil in a heavy pan. Stir in semolina and simmer, stirring frequently, for fifteen to twenty minutes, or until mixture is thick and semolina well cooked. Remove from heat and allow to cool slightly.

4 Whisk egg yolks with castor sugar until thick and light; beat into semolina mixture, together with cream, vanilla and lemon juice.

5 Butter a decorative 2½ pint mould.

6 Whisk egg whites until stiff but not dry. Fold into semolina mixture gently but thoroughly. Pour into mould and chill until set.

7 To serve: turn mould out on to a large, flat serving dish (see p.224). Pour blackcurrant sauce over the top and serve immediately.

Pineapple cream

Serves 6

½oz powdered gelatine
¼ pint pineapple juice, fresh or canned
6 egg yolks
6oz granulated sugar
1 level tablespoon cornflour
¾ pint milk
5 egg whites
Generous pinch of salt
1 level tablespoon castor sugar
3 tablespoons lemon juice
¼ pint double cream, chilled
3–4 slices pineapple, fresh or canned, shredded
Pineapple rings, maraschino cherries and angelica 'leaves', to decorate

The addition of stiffly beaten egg whites turns this delicate sweet into a cross between a Bavarian cream and a cold soufflé. To make an orange cream, substitute orange juice for pineapple juice and intensify the flavour with the freshly grated zest of 2 large oranges.

1 Sprinkle powdered gelatine over pineapple juice and leave to soften.

2 In a large bowl, whisk egg yolks with sugar until fluffy and lemon-coloured; add cornflour and continue to whisk until smoothly blended.

3 Scald milk; add to egg yolk mixture in a thin stream, beating vigorously with the whisk. Then pour into top of double saucepan and cook over simmering water, stirring frequently. As soon as

custard coats back of spoon, plunge base of pan into cold water to arrest cooking process. Do not under any circumstances allow custard to boil, or egg yolks will curdle.

4 Add gelatine and pineapple juice mixture to hot custard, stirring until completely melted. Pour custard into a large bowl.

5 Beat egg whites with salt until soft peaks form. Add castor sugar and continue to beat to a stiff meringue. Fold gently but thoroughly into hot custard mixture and flavour to taste with lemon juice. Flavour should be rather sharp. Allow mixture to become quite cold, drawing a large metal spoon through it occasionally to prevent it separating.

6 When custard mixture is on the point of setting, whip chilled cream (by hand for maximum volume) until floppy and with the same consistency as the pineapple custard mixture. Fold into custard, together with shredded pineapple.

7 Rinse a 3 pint mould with cold water, shaking out all excess. Fill to the brim with pineapple cream; cover with greaseproof paper and chill until firmly set, preferably overnight.

8 To serve: dip mould into very hot water for one second only and turn out on to a flat serving dish. Decorate with halved pineapple rings, maraschino cherries and angelica 'leaves', and return to refrigerator until ready to serve.

Rice à la royale

Serves 8
6oz short-grain rice
6 level tablespoons granulated sugar
$2\frac{1}{4}$ pints milk
3 level tablespoons cornflour
6 egg yolks
7 level tablespoons castor sugar
$\frac{3}{4}$oz powdered gelatine
1–$1\frac{1}{2}$ teaspoons vanilla essence
6 level tablespoons double cream
3–4 tablespoons Kirsch

To decorate
3–4 small, ripe dessert pears, halved, cored and poached in
   light syrup or brushed with lemon juice
Whipped cream
Glacé cherries, halved
Angelica 'leaves'

1 Put (unwashed) rice in a heavy, medium-sized pan. Cover with
   cold water to come 2in above rice. Bring to the boil; stir to dislodge
   any grains stuck to the pan and simmer for five minutes.

2 Drain rice thoroughly in a colander. Return to the pan. Add
   granulated sugar and half the milk. Bring to simmering point,
   stirring frequently, and simmer gently, uncovered, until rice is soft
   and most of the milk has been absorbed, about twenty minutes.
   Remove pan from heat; cover and allow to cool.

3 Blend cornflour to a smooth, thin paste with a little of the
   remaining milk. Then combine cornflour mixture with all the
   remaining milk in the top of a double saucepan. Bring to the boil
   over direct heat and simmer gently for five minutes, stirring
   constantly. Remove from heat.

4 Combine egg yolks and castor sugar in a bowl, and whisk until
   light and fluffy. Add cornflour sauce in a thin stream, whisking.
   Return mixture to top of double saucepan.

5 Fit top part of pan over base containing simmering water and cook,
   stirring frequently, for about twenty minutes, or until custard is
   thick enough to coat back of spoon. Remove from heat and allow
   to cool, beating occasionally to prevent a skin forming on top.

6 Sprinkle gelatine over 4 or 5 tablespoons cold water in a cup and
   leave to soften.

7 When custard is cold, place cup containing gelatine in a bowl of
   hot water and stir until gelatine has completely dissolved. Beat
   gelatine into custard and flavour to taste with vanilla essence.

8 Combine custard with cooked rice mixture, cream and Kirsch, to
   taste.

9 Pour mixture into a deep, round, 3 pint mould. Chill until firmly set, preferably overnight.

10 To unmould rice: dip mould for just one or two seconds into very hot water. Place a large serving dish on top; invert and gently shake rice mould out on to dish. Decorate with halved and cored pears which you have poached in a light syrup or, if they are really ripe and soft, simply brushed all over with lemon juice to prevent discolouration. Finish decoration with swirls of piped whipped cream, halved glacé cherries and 'leaves' cut out of angelica. Serve very cold.

Charlotte Russe à l'orange

Serves 6
Sponge finger biscuits, or strips of sponge cake
½oz powdered gelatine
8–9 juicy oranges (see Step 4)
3 sugar lumps
4 tablespoons lemon juice
6oz granulated sugar
3 eggs, separated
3 level tablespoons castor sugar
½ pint double cream
Vanilla essence (optional)
Lightly sweetened whipped cream and orange segments, to decorate

A classic French mould for a *charlotte Russe* is made of metal, with plain, slightly sloping sides, and two little heart-shaped handles. You can also use a soufflé dish or any other mould with tall, plain sides and a flat bottom.

When it comes to lining the mould, you can choose between sponge finger biscuits and strips of sponge cake. If you use sponge fingers, they will fit better (and the finished result is more attractive if you alternate brown and white sides on the outside). If you have difficulty making them stand up around the sides, try brushing them with a little egg white to hold them in place.

1 Line base of a $2\frac{1}{2}$ to 3 pint charlotte mould with a circle of dampened greaseproof paper. Line sides of mould with a tight layer of sponge fingers (see note above).

2 Sprinkle gelatine over 3 tablespoons cold water in a cup and put aside to soften.

3 Scrub 2 oranges and dry them. Rub sugar lumps all over their zest until thoroughly impregnated with orange oil.

4 Squeeze oranges to make $\frac{3}{4}$ pint strained juice. Combine with lemon juice in the top of a double saucepan.

5 Add sugar lumps and granulated sugar, and stir over direct heat until sugar has dissolved. Do not boil juices as this tends to make them bitter.

6 In a bowl, whisk egg yolks until frothy. Gradually pour in hot juices, whisking vigorously.

7 Return mixture to top of double saucepan and cook over simmering water, stirring, until slightly thickened, ten to fifteen minutes. Remove from heat and allow to cool.

8 Meanwhile, stand bowl containing gelatine in the hot water remaining in the bottom of the double saucepan and stir until thoroughly dissolved. Mix with cooling orange 'custard'. Leave until quite cold but not set.

9 In a medium-sized bowl, whisk egg whites until stiff but not dry. Gradually whisk in castor sugar, and continue to whisk to a stiff, glossy meringue.

10 Slowly add cold orange mixture, whisking vigorously.

11 In another bowl, whisk cream lightly until barely thick enough to hold a trail. Fold in orange mixture and flavour, if liked, with a few drops of vanilla essence. Leave until on the point of setting.

12 When orange cream is very thick, pour into sponge-lined mould and leave in a cool place until set.

To turn out: with a pair of scissors, snip off tips of sponge fingers level with top of filling. If charlotte has stuck to mould, dip briefly in and out of very hot water. Turn out on to a flat serving dish. Remove paper.

Decorate charlotte with lightly sweetened whipped cream and, if liked, orange segments.

Crown of apples

Serves 6–8
Melted butter
¾lb sugar
Spiral of thinly pared lemon zest
A piece of vanilla pod, split, or vanilla essence
¾ pint water
4lb firm, tart dessert apples, e.g. Coxes or Golden Delicious
Crème Anglaise (p.210), to serve

Glaze
6 level tablespoons apricot jam
1 tablespoon apple syrup
1 tablespoon brandy, Kirsch, etc., or lemon juice

Brush a plain, 2 pint ring mould with melted butter.

In a large, heavy pan, combine sugar, lemon zest and vanilla pod, if used (but not vanilla essence), with ¾ pint water. Bring to the boil over a low heat, stirring until sugar has melted; then lower heat to a simmer. If using vanilla essence, do not add it until syrup is simmering to minimise evaporation.

Prepare two apples at a time by cutting them into quarters, coring and peeling them, and slicing them about ⅛in thick. As soon as they are ready, drop slices into simmering syrup and poach for five minutes, or until translucent and soft but not disintegrating. Remove slices from syrup with a slotted spoon and spread out on a plate to cool.

Prepare remaining apples in the same way.

5 Arrange poached apple slices in regular, overlapping circles, close together and with the peeled side of the slices towards the outside edge of the mould. Press each layer lightly with the back of a spoon to 'settle' it.

6 When mould is full, cover tightly with foil and chill overnight.

7 The following day, prepare a glaze by melting apricot jam with a tablespoon of the apple poaching syrup in a small, heavy pan over a low heat. Sieve into a bowl. Cool slightly and flavour with brandy, Kirsch, or a few drops of lemon juice, to taste.

8 Dip ring mould into hot water for just a second to loosen apples, and turn it out on to a large, flat serving dish.

9 Brush apple ring with warm apricot glaze, taking care not to dislodge slices. Chill until ready to serve.

10 Use a sharp knife to slice crown of apples into portions, and serve with a light *crème Anglaise*.

Index